Bead chic

36 Stylish Jewelry Projects and Inspired Variations

Margot Potter

NORTH LIGHT BOOKS

North Light Books
CINCINNATI, OHIO

fwmedia   www.fwmedia.com

14 13 12 11 10   5 4 3 2 1

DISTRIBUTED IN CANADA BY FRASER DIRECT
100 Armstrong Avenue
Georgetown, ON, Canada L7G 5S4
Tel: (905) 877-4411

DISTRIBUTED IN THE U.K. AND EUROPE BY DAVID & CHARLES
Brunel House, Newton Abbot, Devon, TQ12 4PU, England
Tel: (+44) 1626 323200, Fax: (+44) 1626 323319
Email: postmaster@davidandcharles.co.uk

DISTRIBUTED IN AUSTRALIA BY CAPRICORN LINK
P.O. Box 704, S. Windsor NSW, 2756 Australia
Tel: (02) 4577-3555

Library of Congress Cataloging in Publication Data
Potter, Margot.
  Bead chic : 36 stylish jewelry projects and inspired variations / by Margot Potter. -- 1st ed.
     p. cm.
  Includes index.
  ISBN 978-1-4403-0315-9 (pbk. : alk. paper)
  1. Beadwork. 2. Jewelry making. I. Title.
  TT860.P678 2010
  745.58'2--dc22
                                        2010000515

Metric Conversion Chart

To convert	to	multiply by
Inches	Centimeters	2.54
Centimeters	Inches	0.4
Feet	Centimeters	30.5
Centimeters	Feet	0.03
Yards	Meters	0.9
Meters	Yards	1.1

For Avalon

This book is dedicated to my lovely daughter, Avalon, who once again gave up her summer fun so Mom could work on a new book. Thank you for your invaluable help keeping mommy organized and for being my part-time model and design assistant. You will never know just how much it means to me to have such a delightful, funny, smart and talented young muse to make my studio sunny even on the darkest of days. I hope that in some small way I've inspired you to dream big and dare to make those dreams real. I love you more than words can say.

With Gratitude

To my ever patient husband, Drew, I say thank you yet again for supporting my efforts to do the impossible.

Thank you to the folks from Beadalon for your ongoing and ever-appreciated support. Thank you to Homer, Joe and Ronda of HHH Enterprises for everything you do to make the world and my world a better place. Thank you to Steve and the gang from ArtBeads for your gracious support, the team from Auntie's Beads for supporting another of my books, Dave, Russ, Amy and Bill from Rings n Things for getting my request out so efficiently and quickly and to Heather of The Beadin' Path for the absolutely delicious sampling of vintage plastic beads. Thank you to Iliana of Blue Moon Beads for the inspirational samples! Thanks to the folks from Plaid for the fabulous Plaid components. Thanks to Beads World and Phoenix Beads for your support.

To everyone who has supported me online and in the real world—thank you! I have some of the coolest fans on the planet and I am so thrilled to offer you some fresh inspiration.

Who Did What

Editor: Julie Hollyday

Designer: Steven Peters

Production: Greg Nock

Photography: Christine Polomsky, Ric Deliantoni

Stylists: Jan Nickum, Cass Smith, Monica Skrzelowski

About the Author

Impatient, imperfect and impetuous, Margot Potter is a design expert for the rest of us. She's also an author, freelance writer, consultant, public speaker, actor, vocalist and TV Host who creates innovative designs for major manufacturers and magazines, has written five popular humorous how-to books and teaches popular seminars and classes at stores and major craft and jewelry industry events. She's a member of the Beadalon Design Team, a Ranger Ink certified instructor and an ambassador for Create Your Style with CRYSTALLIZED™-Swarovski Elements. She approaches everything with her signature sense of humor, boundless curiosity and copious amounts of *joie de vivre* because she feels that if it's not fun, it's simply not worth doing. She invites people not only to think outside of the box, but to tear it up, repurpose it into something fabulous and stand on it to reach for the stars. She's equally comfortable at the writer's desk, in the design studio, onstage or in front of the camera.

About the Contributors

I cannot thank enough the immensely talented designers who agreed to be involved in this book on such short notice, and for the depth and breadth their creations have added to this effort. We are nothing without our friends, and I am a woman deeply blessed with some truly amazing friends.

Angela Bannatyne
avenueacollection.com

Melanie Brooks
www.earthenwoodstudio.com

Jean Campbell
www.jeancampbellink.com

Tonia Davenport
toniadavenport.typepad.com

Cathie Filian
www.cathiefilian.com

Tammy Powley
www.tammypowley.com

Jean Yates
www.prettykittydogmoonjewelry.com

Jennifer Heynen
Jangles
P.O. Box 82357
Athens, GA 30608
www.jangles.net

Melissa J. Lee
www.strandsofbeads.blogspot.com
www.melissajlee.etsy.com

Rebecca Peck
www.fiskateers.com/blog/author/rebecca

Brenda Pinnick
Brenda Pinnick Designs
www.brendapinnick.com

Barbe Saint John
Saints and Sinners
barbesaintjohn.com

Andrew Thornton
www.andrew-thornton.blogspot.com

Contents

Chapter One

Scale

Chapter Two

Color

5

Introduction

The dilemma for the beader attempting to reproduce a design in a book, catalog or magazine is that finding the exact beads used can be well-nigh impossible. Quite literally, there are millions upon millions of beads from which to choose. So what to do if something catches your eye, but you just can't seem to find that one bead? Or what if you like the idea, but you're not sold on the materials? Well, my dear, fret not!

You can move beyond the "monkey see, monkey do" mind-set and trust your design instincts. You don't have to follow the beader; you can borrow their compass and forge your own creative path. Find designs that delight your eye and tickle your fancy, and make them your own. You can do it and I will show you how.

Think of it as a dialog between you and the designer. What can you add to the conversation? Designs should be springboards for your creativity, not rigid rules that you must slavishly follow. Beads, findings and wire are ever-changing: styles and colors ebbing and flowing, fashion shifting and techniques evolving.

As I was contemplating the aforementioned problem, I wondered what would happen if I created fashion-friendly designs and then reinterpreted them, changing colors, textures, patterns and materials. Instead of cooking with the same ingredients, I'd start with the same recipe, but add a dash, sprinkle or taste of something different. Would it result in delicious designs or distasteful disasters? You will have to decide for yourself.

My goal is to inspire you to be creative. I know you're busy and I know you're crafting in the spaces in between. I want to make those spaces richer and more fulfilling. I'm here to give you solid technique advice and the creative tools you can use to free your vivid imagination. Think of this as a beaded jewelry recipe book. Jot down notes. Add your own variations and original ideas. Before you know it, you'll be a master designer!

xoxo

Margot

Material Matters

You have to gather up a whole lot of shiny and not so shiny things if you want to make jewelry. This section discusses what you need to recreate the projects in this book. And it's only the beginning, because once you start making jewelry, you're going to find yourself asking, "Can I use that to make jewelry?" on a daily basis.

A Strong Foundation: Wire, Chain and Stringing Materials

Hard Wire

Hard wires are used for a wide variety of applications in basic jewelry making. You can use wire to make your own findings. You can use wire to wrap around foundation items or to create jewelry components, and you can use hard wire to give structure to a design.

Hard wire comes in a variety of materials, finishes, gauges, strengths and shapes. Gauge refers to the width of the wire; the smaller the number, the thicker the wire is. Softer materials make a more malleable wire, which is ideal for wrapping and forming around a base. Harder materials are often well suited as structural elements or to make hooks and other findings that will need to withstand more abuse.

Memory wire is tempered steel and will retain its shape, so it can't be wrapped or bent easily and is best used as a foundation. You should never, ever cut memory mire with anything but memory wire shears, because it will destroy the wire cutters.

Sterling silver and copper wires are very soft and easy to manipulate. Steel and iron wires are strong and sturdy, but malleable enough to make great hooks and wrapped elements. You must treat color-coated wire with care so as not to remove the color when manipulating the wire.

Each wire has unique properties and resistance, and the more you explore a variety of them, the more you'll learn about their potential and limitations.

Beading Wire

Beading wire is created from cabled metal that has been coated with nylon. The higher the strand count, the softer and more fluid the wire will be.

The most commonly used diameter is .018, but it's not a rule. This wire comes in a variety of diameters, and it's important to use the thickest diameter to fill the holes in your beads. I use 19-strand or higher in my designs; I find 7-strand is usually too stiff and doesn't achieve the drape I like.

There are sterling silver, silver-plated and gold-plated wires as well as metallic-colored wires and each has its own properties. I love using metallic and vibrantly colored soft wires for woven exposed wire designs; you don't always have to hide the wires because they can become an architectural decorative element in your designs.

Chain

Over the past few years, chain has had a huge resurgence in popularity among jewelry designers. That's great news for all of us because it means our selection is far more varied and prevalent.

Chain brings texture to designs and it can, depending on the style and size, either have a very delicate appeal or a bold edge. I'm currently a fan of gunmetal and aged brass chain, but I also love shiny silver and gold plated. There is such a great variety out there at the moment, it's a good time to stock up and play.

Leather, Waxed Linen, Silk and Ribbon

These materials are great for knotted or exposed designs.

To work with silk, you'll need the help of an awl or a bead-knotter tool, which allows you to knot close to your beads. Leather and linen can be knotted easily by hand. I love the rustic appeal of leather and linen, but I also like the drape and elegance of knotted silk.

Ribbon and rattail can add another dimension to your designs. You can also knot, wrap and tie these materials onto a core strand for dimension and textural interest.

Gather a variety of these materials in different colors and diameters, and see how much fun you can have switching things up.

String 'Em Up! Pendants, Beads and Metal

Millions of styles of pendants, beads and metal elements are available to the designer at bead shows, local bead shops, large craft chains and online jewelry-making Web sites. If you can't find the exact bead pictured in a project, the odds are in your favor that with a little ingenuity and imagination you'll find a perfect stand-in. Here's a rundown of pendants, beads and metal elements, and a few examples of how substituting one bead for another can give your designs a fabulous flair.

Beads

Brilliant, beautiful and beguiling, beads are endlessly fascinating. Made from a litany of materials from glass to metal to plastic to gemstone to shell to nuts to clay—if you can drill a hole in it and string it on a wire or strand, you can call it a bead.

You will never run out of beads to enjoy, and each bead has a unique personality. The size and shape and weight of your beads are important to consider when you're designing. Durability is as important as style. Here's an overview of some of the kinds of beads we'll explore in this book.

Glass and Crystal

Glass and crystal beads are some of the most versatile and interesting beads available to the designer.

Many glass beads are handmade using a variety of methods including lampwork, cane, millefiori, dichroic and handblown.

CRYSTALLIZED-Swarovski Elements are made from precision-cut fine crystal using meticulously crafted color formulas and finishes.

Czech glass beads come in a variety of finishes, color mixes, shapes and styles. The pressed glass shapes add a sense of whimsy to your work.

A wide array of glass beads come from India and China, but the most legendary handcrafted glass is arguably from the Murano region in Italy. Glass beads have a nice weight that works well with a variety of foundations.

Wood and Organic Materials

I use a variety of organic materials in my work: wood beads, buri nut beads, tagua nut slices and shell beads all add something different to the mix. Plus, many of these materials have the same large-and-lightweight advantage often found with plastic beads.

Art Beads

There is an ever-expanding community of bead artists across the globe and the common thread is their passion for creating beads.

The materials and styles these artists incorporate are endless and their work can infuse your work with immense beauty. Some of the more popular materials used include glass, ceramic, pewter, precious metal clay, bronze clay, porcelain, resin and metal.

There is nothing like walking a big bead show where you can meet the artists and get the story behind their designs, and if you get the opportunity I highly recommend that you seize it.

Plastic

I'm a big fan of plastic beads. Vintage materials like Lucite and Bakelite are highly collectible these days, but there are also a lot of great new plastic beads on the market. There are some pretty resin beads coming out of Indonesia.

The best thing about plastic beads is that they are super lightweight, so you can pile them on and never feel weighed down.

Gemstone

Gemstone beads can range immensely in price and quality. There is so much gem material on the bead market it can become overwhelming, but don't fret. It's a great idea to get a reputable book on gemology and educate yourself so you know how to spot good gemstones in a sea of mediocrity. There are lots of reputable sources you can turn to for quality beads. I love the organic feel gemstones give my work.

Pendants and Focal Elements

When looking for good pendants or creating focal elements for your designs, it's important to search out items that have visual impact but also work well with complementary materials. Some pendants are so bold and so distinctive they don't need much more than a simple chain or choker. I look for focal pendants that have elements I can mine for a cohesive finished design. Distinct color combinations or textures or motifs can be great springboards for new directions in your work. Don't be afraid to use nonjewelry items in your work. I used a rusty keyhole to make a flirty pendant in this book and I'm simply mad for how it turned out.

Metal Elements and Charms

Metal, like chain, has surged in popularity recently. Stamping, bending, hammering and oxidizing sheet metal, charms and shapes are great ways to personalize your designs. It's not hard to do and once you start hammering on metal, you might find it hard to stop! Cast-metal charms can also add a lot of dimension, texture and personality to your work.

Fantastic Findings

Findings are the bits and pieces used to connect and create finished jewelry. They include clasps, head and eye pins, earring components, pin backs, jump rings and all of those other small items that make the wire and beads into jewelry designs. Here's a look at what you'll need for the projects in this book.

Head Pins and Eye Pins

These metal pins are used for creating beaded dangles and connectors. A head pin has a flat end that prevents the bead from sliding off. Sometimes these ends can be decorative. An eye pin has a looped end and is used to connect beaded elements in earrings, cascading segments and chains.

Jump Rings

Jump rings create connections. They can also be used as decorative elements in your designs. They come in a variety of sizes, finishes and textures. If you learn how to close jump rings properly, they're a very secure way to add movement to your designs.

Clasps

The jewelry designer has a huge array of choices when it comes to clasps. The basic clasps include spring ring, lobster claw, hook-and-eye, slide clasps, magnetic and S-hook shapes. Beadalon has some great new options for clasps that include Scrimps and EZ-Crimp ends. In this book, you'll also see clasps that both secure a design and act as a decorative element.

Ear Wires

Ear wires are used to attach an earring to a pierced earlobe. They also come in a wide variety of styles from the simple shepherd's hook and kidney, to the more ornate French wire, chandelier components and the popular lever-back style. Ear wires can be decorative or very simple.

Crimp Tubes

A crimp is a metal bead or tube that you use to connect beading wire to a clasp. Using a special tool called a crimp tool, you can attach the wire to your clasp easily and securely. I do not recommend using chain-nose pliers to flatten crimps because it can compromise the nylon coating on the beading wire. Crimp beads and tubes come in an array of sizes, textures and finishes.

EZ-Crimps

The EZ-Crimp is a Beadalon innovation that is easier to use than a traditional crimp bead or tube. The wire is inserted into a chamber and the metal is compressed securely around it with a special tool. This secures the wire for beading. As you will soon discover, I'm a huge fan of this finding.

Wire Guardians

Over time, the friction from wearing your beaded jewelry can wear the nylon coating from the wire and eventually can cause the wire to break. Wire guardians are little metal tubes used to protect your bead wire from wearing against the metal on the clasp or jump ring. They are particularly useful for watches, bracelets and designs with heavier beads.

11

Crimp Covers

Split metal beads called crimp covers are used to conceal the crimps at the end of jewelry designs. They're very easy to use and create a clean finish. Use an EZ-Crimp tool or a Mighty Crimp tool to close them around the crimp beads. Crimp covers work only with crimps that are size 2 and smaller.

Quick Links

These ingenious flat textured or smooth metal links from Beadalon, with easy-to-use connectors, make quick work of jewelry design. They come in an assortment of shapes and sizes and are a great way to get your creative juices flowing.

Tool Time

Every endeavor is made easier and more efficient by the proper tools. I'll show you some of the basics and delve into a few you may not have used before. I always recommend buying the best quality tools you can afford. Good materials and foundations are made even stronger with the best tools and well-executed techniques.

The Right Stuff: Basic Jewelry-Making Tools

These are the go-to tools for most of the techniques you'll need to make basic jewelry with hard and soft wire, beads and metal blanks.

Round-Nose Pliers

These pliers have conical jaws that are used to create loops and round bends in hard wire. The finer the tip, the better the pliers and the easier they will be to use effectively. For best results, work close to the end of the pliers; if you want to make larger loops, however, slide down the jaws.

Chain-Nose Pliers

These pliers have flat, textured jaws that are ideal for grasping, tugging and tucking hard wire. Again, try to find a pair with finer tips for best results. You can purchase a coating medium for the tips or nylon-jaw pliers that will help prevent nicking and marring your hard wire.

Flush Cutters

Flush cutters are used to cut hard and soft wire and leave an angled cut on one side of the wire and a flush cut on the other. It's important to read the packaging to see what strength, gauge and type of wire they are intended to cut, otherwise, you may quickly destroy your cutters. When you cut jump rings, be sure to go back and recut the angled side so you have two flush ends that will close easily.

Memory Wire Shears

These shears are specifically designed to cut the tempered steel used for memory wire. It's important that you use these and not flush cutters on memory wire or any steel or iron wire.

Crimp Tool

A crimp tool is used to secure a metal bead or tube that attaches the wire to a clasp to prepare it for beading. Crimping is an important skill to master. It's also important to remember that there are different sizes of crimp beads and tubes, and three different sizes of crimp tools to accommodate them: Micro Crimp Tool, crimp tool and Mighty Crimp Tool.

EZ-Crimp Tool

I use a fun gadget called an EZ-Crimp Tool throughout this book. You use it to compress a tube component that secure yours wire for beading. You can also use a Mighty Crimp Tool for this purpose, but a regular crimp tool won't be big enough to accommodate the EZ-Crimp ends.

Chasing or Ball-Peen Hammer

This handy little hammer is a great tool for your hard wire and metalworking arsenal. One end is round, ideal for hammering texture, and the other flat end is perfect for hammering wire and shapes flat. You can use this hammer in conjunction with a mini anvil or a steel block.

Steel Bench Block

A steel bench block is an extremely hard and durable surface upon which you can hammer, flatten, stamp and straighten metal bits and pieces. For noise control, place a small sandbag under your steel block to muffle the sound it makes when being hammered, or you can simply revel in the percussive moment.

Jump Ring Maker Tool

If you don't already have one of these nifty tools, you should add one to your stash. It makes quick work of wrapping hard wire around a dowel and producing a cache of jump rings in a flash. It has a variety of dowels in different sizes to make a variety of different-sized jump rings.

Metal Stamps

Metal stamps are used in metalworking to permanently stamp numbers, letters or shapes into a surface. Place the item you wish to embellish on your steel bench block or mini anvil and strike hard several times with the chasing hammer to permanently stamp the image into the metal surface.

Sanding Block

A sanding block is used to smooth wire ends of ear wires or clasps. There are a variety of styles, from forms that hold actual sandpaper to foam blocks coated with a sandpaper like surface. These can also be a lot of fun for distressing plastic or paper beads.

Bead Boards, Bead Mats and Tacky Bead Mats

These are great accessories for keeping your beads and findings corralled while you're working on a project. Bead boards not only offer spots to keep beads and findings, they feature channels that will aid you in designing your jewelry. Vellux bead mats offer a smooth but grabbing surface to keep beads from rolling around. The Tacky Bead Mat from Beadalon has a sticky surface perfect for holding small beads and findings.

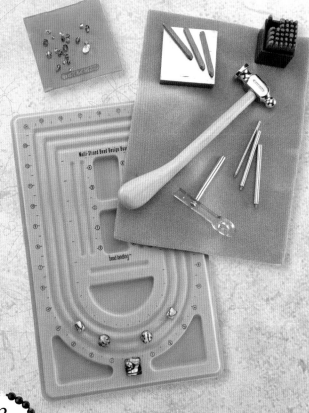

Techniques

Nothing is more important to the success and joy of your jewelry-making endeavors than developing good technique. It's the key to making it fun and easy and, more importantly, to producing jewelry pieces that look professional. Practice truly makes perfect, so practice as often as possible!

Hammering Texture into Wire and Metal

Place the hard wire or metal elements on a steel bench block or mini anvil and use the ball-peen (round) end of a chasing hammer to create texture. The flat end of the hammer flattens the wire.

Turning a Loop

1

2

3

4

1 Thread a bead onto a head pin. Bend the wire at a 90-degree angle flush to the top of the bead.

2 Cut off the excess wire with the wire cutters, leaving a ¼" (6mm) tail.

3 Grasp the tail in the very tip of the round-nose pliers and bend it over itself into a loop.

4 The bead should have a round loop at the top when you are finished. At first your loops will look more like "p's" than "o's", but they will improve as you practice.

Making a Wrapped Loop

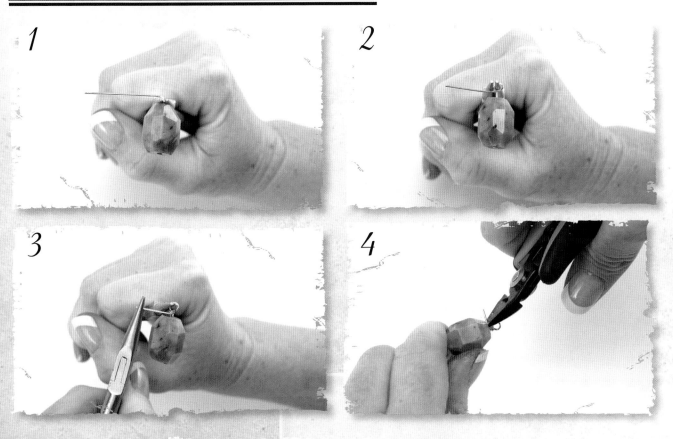

1 **2**

3 **4**

5

1 Thread a bead onto a head pin. With the round-nose pliers, grasp the wire at the top of the bead. Bend the wire at a 90-degree angle to the top of the pliers.

2 Use your fingers or a pair of chain-nose pliers to bend the wire around one of the pincers to form a loop.

3 Use your fingers or chain-nose pliers to firmly coil the wire around the base of the loop until the coiled wire reaches the top of the bead.

4 Cut off the excess wire with the wire cutters.

5 Use the chain-nose pliers to tuck the remaining wire tail into the bottom of the coil.

Wrapping Wire Around a Base

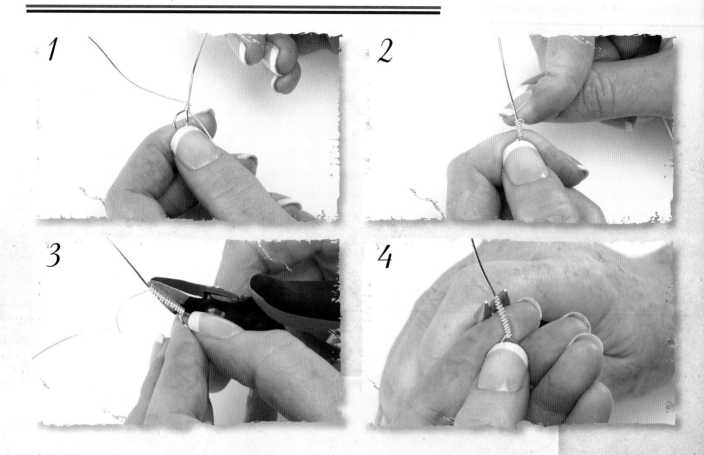

1 Wire wrapping around a base can be done with a wire already attached to the base, or with a wire you add. The wire you wrap around the base is called the "working wire." Wrap the working wire tightly around the end of the base or core wire.

2 Continue wrapping with tension, working up the core wire and using your pointer finger to keep the wire flush as you work.

3 When you reach the desired length, cut off the excess wire with the wire cutters.

4 Use chain-nose pliers to tuck the wire tail under.

Making Ear Wires

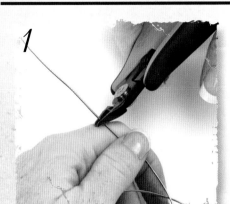

1

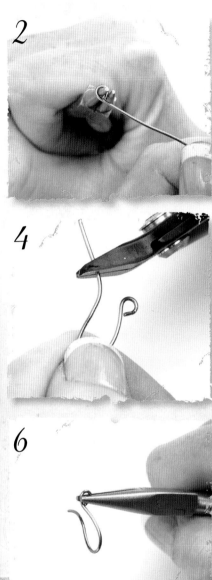

2

3

4

5

6

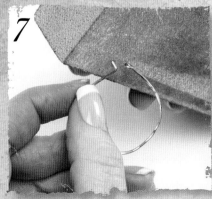

7

1 Cut a 4" (10cm) piece of 18-gauge (or higher) wire.

2 Grasp the end of the wire with round-nose pliers and turn a small loop.

3 Bend the wire over your pointer finger to create a U-shape.

4 Cut off the excess wire, leaving a 1/8" (3mm) tail.

5 Bend the wire tail slightly with your fingers or the round-nose pliers.

6 Use chain-nose pliers to bend the loop upward at a 90-degree angle from the front of the hook.

7 No matter what type of earwire you make, sand the cut wire end to make it more comfortable when passing through the earlobe. Here, I'm sanding a hoop I made from copper wire.

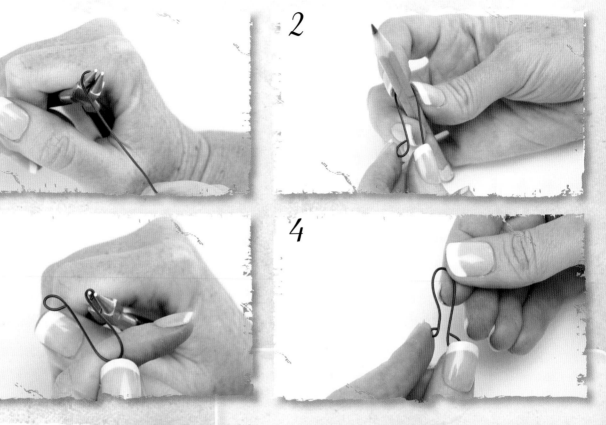

1 After cutting the wire to length (lengths are given in the instructions for the projects), use the inside of the jaws of the round-nose pliers to create a large loop at one end of the wire.

2 Bend the wire over a dowel (a pencil, in this case) to create the hook, using your fingers to adjust the shape.

3 Use the tip of the jaws of the round-nose pliers to create a small loop in the opposite end of the wire.

4 Use your fingers to adjust the shape.

5 Use the flat part of a chasing hammer and a steel bench block to flatten the curved portion of the hook.

Making a Wrapped Wire Hook

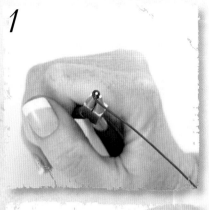

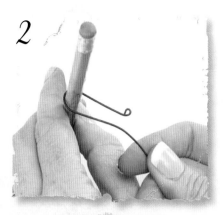

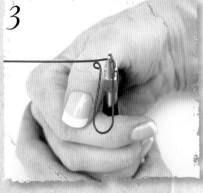

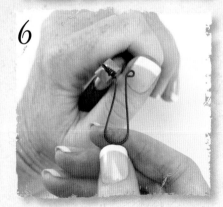

1 After cutting the wire to length (lengths are given in the instructions for the projects), use the tips of the jaws of the round-nose pliers to create a small loop in one end of the wire.

2 Bend the wire over a dowel (a pencil, in this case) to create the hook.

3 Use the round-nose pliers to create a wrapped loop. Start by bending the wire at a 90-degree angle.

4 Loop the wire over one of the jaws of the pliers to create a loop.

5 Wrap the wire tail around the core wire. Secure the loop in the jaws of the round-nose pliers and grip and move the working wire with the chain-nose pliers.

6 Cut off the wire tail with the wire cutters. Use the chain-nose pliers to tuck the excess wire under.

Optional: Use the chasing hammer to flatten the hook, if you desire.

Making Jump Rings

1

2

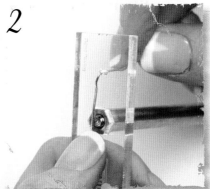

3

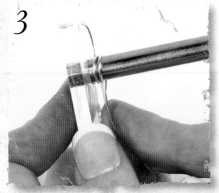

4

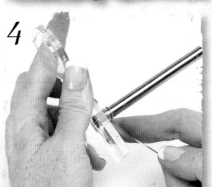

5

6

7

1 Using your jump ring maker tool set, select the dowel in the diameter you want and screw it into the base. Insert the end of the wire you've chosen into the hole on the jump ring maker. Thread from top to bottom.

2 Bend the wire end flush to the bottom of the jump ring maker with your fingers to secure the wire.

3 Begin wrapping the free wire tightly around the dowel, working the wire down as you wrap, wrapping each new coil closely to the previous one.

4 Continue wrapping the wire tightly around the dowel until you reach your desired length.

5 Cut off the secured bent wire with the wire cutters and remove the coil.

6 Use the flush cutters to cut rings.

7 Go back into each ring and cut the pointed end flush using the flush-cutter tool. Doing so ensures that they close properly.

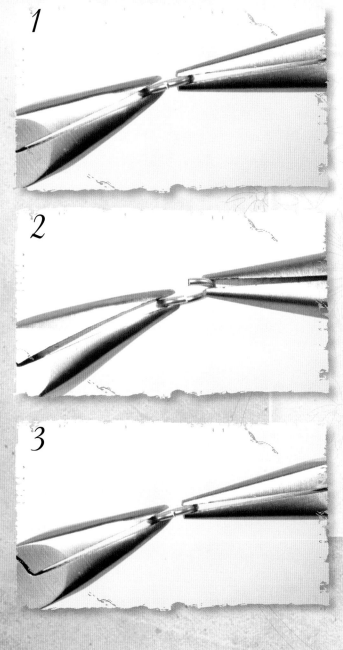

1 Using two pairs of chain-nose pliers, grasp the jump ring on either side of the break in the tips of the jaws of the pliers. (If you don't have two pairs of chain-nose pliers, you can use a pair of bent-nose pliers in place of one of the chain-nose pairs.)

2 The key to opening a jump ring is to move the pliers in opposition to each other instead of outward from the center. If you open a jump ring by pulling the ends apart, the metal become stressed and the circle loses its shape. Open the ring laterally, so that one end is moving toward you and one end is moving away from you.

3 When you are ready to close the jump ring, grasp the ends in your pliers and move them past each other, as you did before, gently compressing them together as you move them. Move the ends past each other again, but this time you should feel them click into place. This means you've created tension and the jump ring should remain closed. If they don't click, keep passing them while gently compressing them until they are secure.

Opening and Closing Chain Links

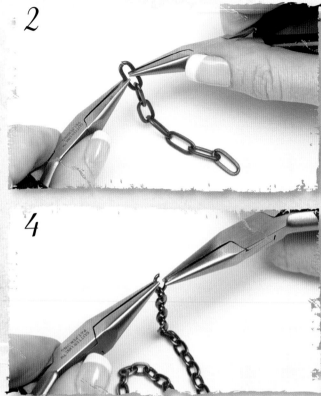

1 Using two pairs of chain-nose pliers, grasp the ends of the chain link on each side of the link opening. Keep your hands and the pliers evenly outstretched on each side of the link; this will give you leverage while you work. Open the links gently and in opposition to each other in a scissor fashion; this will keep the links from losing their shape.

2 Try to close the links with tension, the way you close a jump ring, so they don't open later.

3 Some chain links are soldered shut. You can cut them at the solder point if you are careful.

4 Use the chain-nose pliers as before to open and close the links.

5 Check to make sure the link is secured before you finish.

Making a Rosary-Style Chain

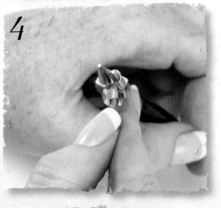
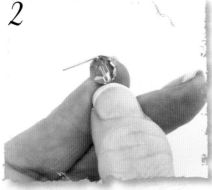

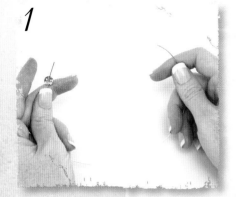

1 Cut off a length of wire. Thread a bead on the wire.

2 Bend about ¼" (6mm) of wire at a 90-degree angle flush to the top of the bead.

3 Grasp the end of the wire with the tips of the round-nose pliers and form a loop.

4 If you work near the tip of your pliers and grasp the wire's tip, you should create a round loop instead of a "p" shape. Practice makes perfect!

5 Bend the wire on the other side of the bead to a 90-degree angle flush to the top of the bead. Cut off the excess wire using the wire cutters, leaving a ¼" (6mm) tail.

6 Create a loop as before. The loop should be at a 90-degree angle from your first loop.

7 Create a second double-looped bead and open one of the loops to thread it into your first bead.

8 Use the chain-nose pliers to close the loop. Continue making and connecting double-looped beads to make a chain.

1

2

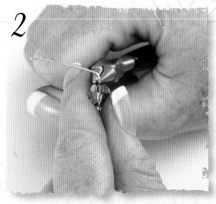

3

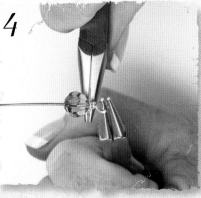

4

5

6

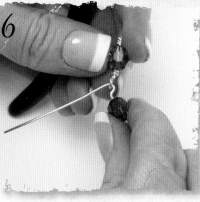

7

8

1 Working from a spool of wire, thread a bead on a core wire and extend the wire about 1" (3cm) from the top of the bead.

2 Grasp the wire at the top of the bead with the round-nose pliers and bend the wire at a 90-degree angle over the pliers.

3 Make a loop with the wire, moving the pliers up as you work. Note the change in position in the photo.

4 Grasp the wire tail with the chain-nose pliers and wrap the wire until it is flush to the top of your bead.

5 Cut off the wire using the wire cutters, and tuck in the tail with the chain-nose pliers.

6 Make another wrapped loop on the opposite side of the bead, measuring as you did in step one and trimming the wire from the spool. Start a second wrapped loop on a second bead and, before you start wrapping, slide the loop into one of the loops on the first bead.

7 Continue wrapping, using the pliers to secure the wire as you work. Cut off the excess wire as needed.

8 Finish the coiled loop on the opposite side of the second bead and continue threading double-coiled beads into one another to make a chain.

Crimping Wire

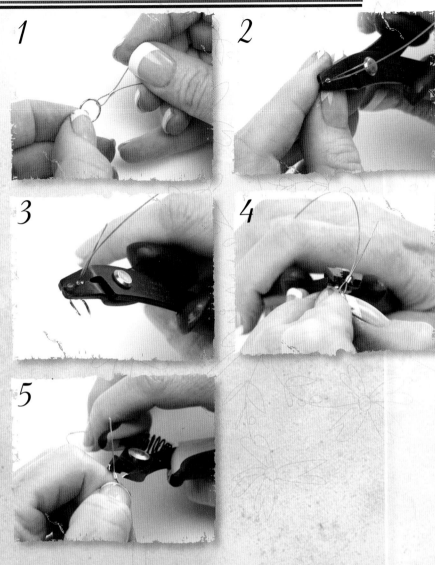

1. Thread the beading wire into the crimp tube, through the clasp and back through the crimp tube.

2. Although the wires will tend to cross, use your thumb to keep them uncrossed so you don't compromise the strength of the crimp-to-clasp connection. Place the tube inside the large hole at the front of the crimp tool and compress it into an oval shape. The oval shape helps keep the wires separated before the final crimping step.

3. Place the oval tube into the indented hole at the back end of the crimp tool and compress the tube, creating a separate chamber for each wire.

4. Place the flattened crimp tube back into the large hole at the front end of the crimp tool with the smooth side facing the inside jaws of the pliers. Compress the ends together, folding the tube in half.

5. Use the wire cutters to cut the excess wire tail flush to the bottom of the crimped tube.

Crimping Wire with an EZ-Crimp End

1. Thread the end of the wire into the EZ-Crimp end. Place the EZ-Crimp end into the large hole of a Mighty Crimp Tool or an EZ-Crimp Tool. Align the shiny sides of the tube with the jaws of the pliers.

2. Squeeze the handles of the tool to compress the tube around the wire, pressing hard while working up and down the tube. Test the wire to be sure it is secure. Continue squeezing until the wire is secure.

Chapter 1

Scale

It's amazing how much changing the scale of a design changes its overall appearance. Perhaps you love a necklace you see in a magazine, but it seems a bit too large for your tastes. It's not so hard to take that basic idea and rework it with smaller beads or a thinner chain. After you master the basics of jewelry making, the only limit to your designs are the laws of physics.

In this chapter, we'll explore how changing the scale of your materials affects the finished design. You'll learn how to reinterpret ideas to suit your needs. How many times have you come across a piece of jewelry and thought to yourself, "If only that was a little bigger, just a bit longer or a tad shorter?" Now you'll know how to make your jewelry work for you.

Scale is a very important part of the design process, and we're going to explore it fully here. With just a few adjustments and a little ingenuity, you'll be able to make jewelry that works for every outfit and every season. What fun!

"What is art but life upon the larger scale, the higher? When, graduating up in a spiral line of still expanding and ascending gyres, it pushes toward the intense significance of all things, hungry for the infinite." Elizabeth Barrett Browning

Chaos in Pearls

Crystal pearls, faceted plastic rounds and gunmetal chains are clustered in a chaotic mass at the front of this daring, delightful and decidedly different necklace design. The less you map this one out, the better. You can opt to vary the chain lengths even more dramatically to give it an *haute couture* flair.

MATERIALS

- 13 8mm black plastic faceted rounds
- 14 12mm CRYSTALLIZED-Swarovski Elements cream pearls
- 39 1½"–3" (4cm–7.5cm) lengths small gunmetal curb chain
- 18½" (47cm) section gunmetal oval rolo chain
- 27 gunmetal head pins
- 1 large silver-plated swivel lobster clasp
- 15 4mm gunmetal jump rings
- round-nose pliers
- 2 pairs chain-nose pliers
- wire cutters

28

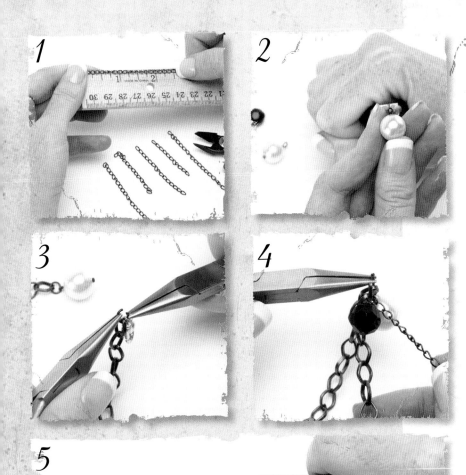

1 Using the wire cutters, cut the small curb chain into 39 separate chains, measuring 1½"–3" (4cm–7.5cm) in length.

2 Create looped dangles for every pearl and faceted round using the head pins (see Turning a Loop on page 14).

3 Cut an 18½" (47cm) section of rolo chain. Attach a pearl to one end using a jump ring (see Opening and Closing jump Rings on page 21). Attach the lobster clasp to the other end using a jump ring.

4 Starting on the thirty-second link in the chain, use a jump ring to attach a pearl, a faceted round and three varied lengths of the small chain.

5 Move down every link and repeat attaching a pearl, a round and three varied lengths of chain on a jump ring. In this project, there are 13 pearl, round and chain combos total in the center portion of the rolo chain.

Mod Bubbles

What is the same? I used a cluster of beads and wire circles gathered in the front of the chain, and I incorporated the black plastic rounds again.
What is different? The scale here is much larger, and it changes the feel of the design. I also added vibrant colors in the plastic rounds and used black, instead of gunmetal, chain. The flower circles from Beadalon replace the dangling chains for a mod vibe.

Autumnal Necklace

Sumptuous multihued rondelles are the perfect complement to aged copper chain. I've added a single, pretty copper filigree to this asymmetrical design for balance. This necklace is as sure to please on a cool fall evening, as it is to delight on a hot summer night.

MATERIALS

23 multicolored turquoise rondelles

1 copper leaf branch filigree

23½" (60cm) section large oval aged copper chain

23 copper head pins

large copper lobster clasp

6 6mm copper jump rings

round-nose pliers

2 pairs chain-nose pliers

wire cutters

1 Choose one end of the chain and count in 5 links. Attach the opposite end of the chain to the fifth link using a jump ring (see Opening and Closing Jump Rings on page 21). This creates a 5-link section and a double-chain section.

2 Create 6 coiled dangles using varied colored rondelles (see Making a Wrapped Loop on page 15). I've made long coils here to showcase the copper. Attach one set of three dangles on a jump ring to the end of the 5-link segment. Save the remaining three for step 5.

3 Create a rosary chain using the rondelles in a variegated color palette (see Making a Rosary-Style Chain on page 23). There is no specific order here, let intuition guide you. (Or make a specific pattern if that makes you happy!)

4 Attach one end of the rosary chain to the fifteenth link on the double chain using a jump ring. Attach the lobster clasp to the other end of the rosary chain. You will use the 5-link segment for the clasp.

5 Attach the 3 coiled dangles to the filigree branch using jump rings.

6 Attach the top of the branch to the bottom jump ring that connects the rosary to the chain.

Sweetheart

What's the same? The pattern is identical but in a much smaller and more delicate scale. See how much changes when you change the size of the beads and components? You can often totally reinterpret a design just by shifting the scale.

What's different? I used small freshwater pearls and tiny garnets in the rosary side of this design. Rather than a large filigree, I featured a tiny sterling silver heart. I used a delicate EZ-Lobster clasp to prevent the design from slipping when it's being worn.

Jacob's Ladder Bracelet

This stunning bracelet is far easier to re-create than it initially appears. Patience is the key as you work along the chains to ensure even spacing of the beaded eye pins.

1

2

3

4

5

6

1 Remove the chain segments (see Opening and Closing Chain Links on page 22). Create wrapped dangles using the head pins and all the gray beads (see Making a Wrapped Loop on page 15).

2 Thread an eye pin into the third link on both chain segments, adding a pink round to the pin after it is inserted into the first chain to create a rung on the beaded ladder.

3 Use round-nose pliers to bend a loop into the exposed end of the eye pin (see Turning a Loop on page 14).

4 Attach a jump ring to each end to prevent the eye pin from sliding back into the chain. Add a wrapped gray dangle to the loop on each side of the eye pin, using the attached jump rings.

Repeat steps 2–4, working down the chain using every other link. Make sure the chains don't twist and stay flat as you work.

5 Attach a jump ring to the last open chain links on the opposite end.

6 Attach the circle end of the toggle clasp to one end of the bracelet. Attach a second jump ring and the bar end of the toggle clasp to the other. Check through the design to ensure all the jump rings are secure.

Fashion forward

Sophistication Earrings

What's the same? I used the same ladder technique to make a fabulous pair of swingy earrings.

What's different? The scale here is much larger. I've only used three beaded links for each earring, and the longer chain segments separate the pearls creating more open space. I attached briolettes on jump rings instead of coiled dangles. By leaving the bottom of each chain separated, you get a lot of movement and interest.

Flight Necklace

An unexpected combination of vibrant colors takes flight in this whimsical but feminine design. The pretty focal pendant inspired the delicate and airy chain. There's a slight asymmetrical quality at work here.

MATERIALS

- 1 metal butterfly pendant
- 4 frosted smoky brown glass flat briolette pendants
- 25 4mm hot pink dyed gemstone rounds
- 25 3mm red dyed gemstone rounds
- 13 4mm faceted hematite rounds
- 1 large silver-plated swivel lobster clasp
- 22-gauge German-style wire
- 8 silver-plated head pins
- 7 6mm silver-plated jump rings
- round-nose pliers
- 2 pairs chain-nose pliers
- wire cutters

1

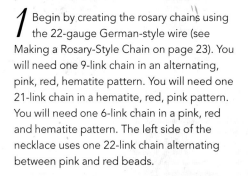

1 Begin by creating the rosary chains using the 22-gauge German-style wire (see Making a Rosary-Style Chain on page 23). You will need one 9-link chain in an alternating, pink, red, hematite pattern. You will need one 21-link chain in a hematite, red, pink pattern. You will need one 6-link chain in a pink, red and hematite pattern. The left side of the necklace uses one 22-link chain alternating between pink and red beads.

2

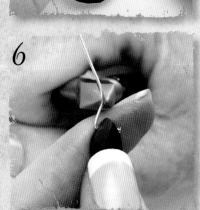

2 Attach a lobster clasp to one end of the 21-link chain using a jump ring (see Opening and Closing Jump Rings on page 21). Attach the shortest chain and the 22-link chain to a jump ring.

3

3 Attach the open end of the 21-link chain, the 9-link chain and the 22-link chain, in that order, to a jump ring. This will create a Y-shape.

4

4 Attach the butterfly to the bottom of the 9-link chain using a jump ring.

5

5 Create two red and two pink looped dangles (see Turning a Loop on page 14). Attach them to the holes at the top left and right of each wing, as shown in the photo.

6

6 Thread a head pin into a briolette. Bend the head pin wire flush to the top of the briolette.

7

7 Use the round-nose and chain-nose pliers to create a wrapped loop (see Making a Wrapped Loop on page 15).

8

9

8 Using the wire cutters, cut off excess wire. Use the chain-nose pliers to tuck in the wire tail and adjust the top loop.

9 Attach the briolettes to the Y-section of the chain under each of the hematite beads using a jump ring.

10 Attach the final briolette to the extension chain at the back of the necklace using a jump ring.

10

Secret Garden

What's the same? I've used the 'Y' and rosary concept on the center and left side of the design. I used the focal pendant as the jumping off point for the design aesthetic.

What's different? I used chain and beads on the right side of the design instead of a rosary chain. The scale is much larger, which makes the piece a little heavier in appearance. The pendant came with its own dangles, so I didn't add any along the 'Y' section and made the 'Y' section a little shorter.

Queen Anne's Lace Earrings

Not for the shy or retiring, these earrings will get you noticed! Wire and beads are loosely wrapped along the edge of a brushed metal frame while a large soft finish acrylic bead with a floral image is accented with a Quick Links circle. These are flirty and fun, a breeze to create and they've got a ton of swingy movement when worn.

MATERIALS

2 Plaid Fresh red acrylic pendants with floral designs

2 Plaid Fresh brushed metal round frames

2 1" (2.5cm) Quick Links rounds

14 4mm black onyx rounds

22-gauge German-style wire

2 French ear wires

6 6mm jump rings

round-nose pliers

2 pairs chain-nose pliers

wire cutters

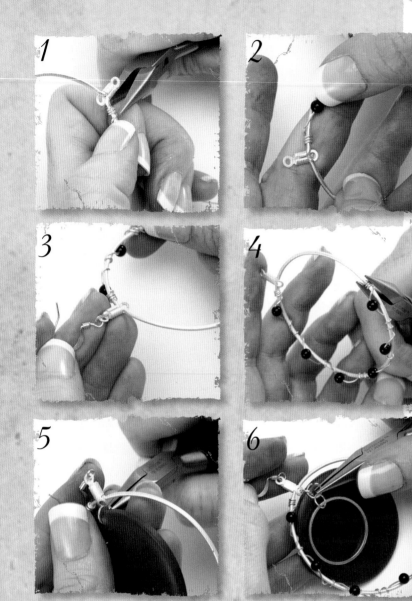

1 Start wrapping one round frame at the top left side with the wire (see Wrapping Wire Around a Base on page 16). Tuck the tail under with chain-nose pliers.

2 Make three tight coils, then string on the first bead. This is a looser wrap, so stretch it out a little.

3 Wrap the wire around the frame twice, with enough tension to secure the bead to the front of the frame, and add the next bead. Continue until you reach the seventh bead. The wire will not go all the way around the frames.

4 Cut the wire and tuck the tail under. Repeat Steps 1–4 for the other earring, beginning at the top right side. Attach the ear wires to the top of the frames.

5 Attach the pendant to the bottom of the frame bail using a jump ring (see Opening and Closing Jump Rings on page 21).

6 Use 2 jump rings to create a chain and add the Quick Link to the bottom ring. Repeat steps 5–6 for the matching earring.

Flora Noir By Cathie Filian

What is the same? The classic color palette of red, black and silver; the circle theme; and the size of the outer hoops are all elements of the Queen Anne's Lace Earrings used for the necklace variation.

What is different? I use much larger black beads for the necklace. I also adjusted the scale of the inner hoop. Instead of using one large hoop, I used lots of smaller jump rings to create a flirty look. I also chose a slightly different inner pendant. The round opening on the pendant enhances the circle theme and allows for an area where the flirty jump rings can dangle.

Steel City Earrings

Annealed iron wire has a dark and mysterious quality that I absolutely love. Faceted freshwater pearls are suspended between the sides of a bent and hammered wire. The bright wire is wrapped in a freeform manner for a cocoon-like appearance. Making these wire segments is surprisingly easy and fun. What other designs can you make with this basic idea?

Design Tip

Play with the wire to get a feel for it. Different wires have different levels of malleability. These earrings do not have to be perfect, so don't sweat it if they aren't!

MATERIALS

- 2 8mm faceted cream freshwater pearls
- 24-gauge silver-plated wire
- 20-gauge annealed iron wire
- 2 gunmetal leverback ear wires
- chasing hammer
- steel bench block
- large round dowel
- small dowel
- memory wire shears
- round-nose pliers
- chain-nose pliers
- wire cutters

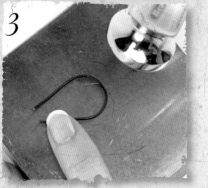

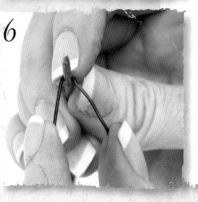

1 Cut a 2½" (6cm) segment of iron wire using the memory wire shears.

2 Bend the center of the wire around the large dowel to create a V-shape (I used the handle of my chasing hammer).

3 Hammer the U-shape flat using the flat end of the chasing hammer.

4 Create a loop in both wire ends (see Turning a Loop on page 14).

5 Cut a ¼" (6mm) section of wire and use the tip of the round-nose pliers to create a very small loop in both ends.

6 Cut a 1¼" (3cm) section of wire and bend it over the metal end of the rattail comb to form a V-shape (I used the metal end of a rattail comb).

7 Use the round-nose pliers to create a loop at both wire ends.

8 Wrap the 24-gauge wire tightly to one side of the top section of the U-shaped component, moving the wire down the core. Continue wrapping the wire around the core in a freeform manner.

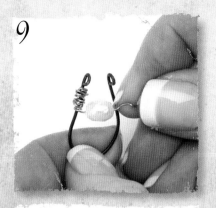

9

10

11

12

13

9 Thread a pearl onto the 24-gauge wire.

10 Tightly wrap the wire around the opposite side, moving up the core in a freeform manner, as before. Cut off the excess wire with the wire cutters and use the chain-nose pliers to tuck the wire tails in.

11 Connect the segments together as follows: Attach the V-shaped component to the loops on the end of the bar component.

12 Attach the U-shaped component to the bar. The loops should all face backward so the components can swing freely when worn.

13 Attach the ear wires to the top of each V-section.

South Beach By Barbe Saint John

What is the same? I mimicked the shaped wire segments.

What is different? Instead of using the triangle segments, I created three graduated sizes of the round segment and attached them together to create a long, flowing earring. I used different gemstone beads to create a South Beach feel.

Fashion forward

Color

Color is, for most people, the most daunting aspect of design to master. The thing is, color is around you every day: It's in your closet, on your walls, in your garden, on your TV, in the magazines you read and on the Web pages you visit. If you begin by going into your closet and assessing your personal palette, you'll find that certain colors resonate for you, and that's a great place to start.

In this chapter, we'll look at designs with unusual color combinations and variations of these designs that show how you can totally change a design by using different colors. I highly recommend getting a color wheel and using it to learn the basic rules of color combinations. Then I recommend designing with those rules in mind for a while. After you feel comfortable with these rules, I suggest you throw them away and go with your intuition. I find that the less I follow rigid rules and the more I trust my intuition, the better my work becomes.

When you learn how to make jewelry, you can create designs that work with any clothing you buy and you're no longer a slave to what's available at retail. This means no more trolling the Internet and trudging the malls to find the perfect necklace to match that fabulous new blouse.

"I found I could say things with color and shapes that I couldn't say any other way—things I had no words for." Georgia O'Keefe

Geometric Necklace

These gemstone spacer beads had been in my bead coffers for a while. When I rediscovered them, I realized that I could, with a little ingenuity, do something totally unexpected with them. By threading them with head pins and glass beads, I created pagoda-like sections that look great in trios.

Design Tip

Don't be afraid to use materials in unexpected and unintended ways. Some of my best work has come from re-imagining jewelry parts. Take risks!

MATERIALS

5 1" × ½" (2.5cm × 1cm) rose quartz oval 3-hole spacers

1 1" × ½" (2.5cm × 1cm) rose quartz rectangle 3-hole pendant

27 4mm striated blue Czech glass rondelles

18 4mm striated raspberry pink Czech glass rondelles

27 4mm hematite tubes

2 5-link segments of silver-colored Quick Links oval chain

19-strand .018 Beadalon wire

2 sterling silver EZ-Crimps

3 ball-tip silver-plated head pins

9 1½" (4cm) silver-plated head pins

3 6mm silver-plated jump rings

EZ-Crimp Tool

round-nose pliers

2 pairs chain-nose pliers

wire cutters

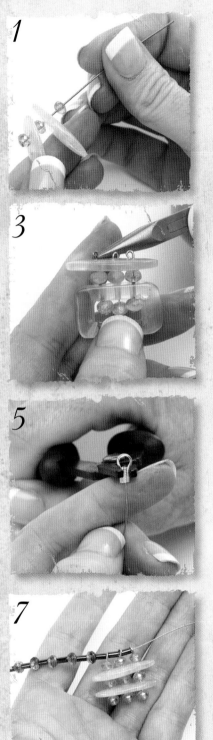

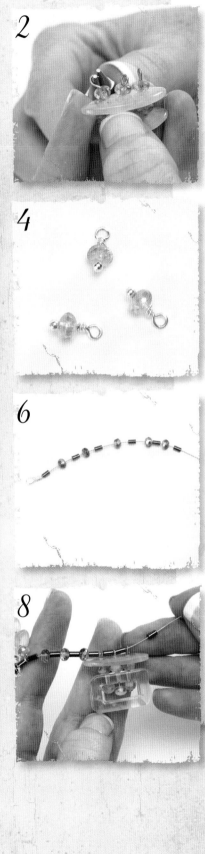

1 Thread a rondelle, the outside hole of a spacer, a rondelle, the outside hole of a second spacer and a third rondelle onto a head pin.

2 Turn a loop flush to the top of the head pin and cut off the excess wire (see Turning a Loop on page 14). Repeat with the other two holes in the spacers.
   Repeat steps 1–2 to make one more of these pendants.

3 Thread a rondelle onto a head pin and slide it into the rectangular pendant on the outside hole, add a rondelle and slide it through a spacer. Loop the top of the head pin flush to the top of the pendant. Repeat for the remaining three holes.

4 Create wrapped dangles with three of the blue rondelles and the ball-tip head pins (see Making a Wrapped Loop on page 15).

5 Attach an EZ-Crimp to one end of a 9" (23cm) segment of Beadalon wire (see Crimping Wire With an EZ-Crimp End on page 25).

6 Add the beads in the following pattern: hematite, pink rondelle, hematite, pink rondelle, hematite, pink rondelle, hematite, pink rondelle, hematite, pink rondelle, hematite, pink rondelle and a hematite.

7 Slide the wire into the loop of one of the double-spacer pendants, adding a hematite tube in between each loop. Then continue alternating four hematites and three pink rondelles.

8 Slide the wire into the rectangle pendant, adding a hematite tube in between each loop.

9

10

11

12

9 Finish alternating between 7 hematite tubes and 6 pink rondelles. Attach the EZ-Crimp, keeping the segment rounded to prevent it from becoming too stiff. Cut off excess wire.

10 Attach the 5-link chain segments by using a jump ring at each EZ-Crimp end on the beaded section (see Opening and Closing Jump Rings on page 21).

11 Attach three beaded dangles to a jump ring. Attach the beaded jump ring to the bottom of the chain on the right side of the necklace.

12 Attach the clasp to the end of the chain on the right side with another jump ring.

Fashion forward

Peas in a Pod

What is the same? I used the three-hole pendant concept and the same hematite tubes.

What is different? I changed the color palette, making it richer and more vintage inspired. It reminds me of a martini! I used wire guardians and crimp covers instead of EZ-Crimps, and the beaded strand is all hematite. The chain is diamond-shaped instead of ovals. These are subtle changes, but somehow the finished effect feels very different.

Mermaid Necklace

I wanted everything in this design to accentuate the beauty of this cast-pewter mermaid pendant from the talented Cynthia Thornton of Green Girl Studios. Two ocean-themed colors and a sprinkling of Hill Tribe silver stick beads combine to make a simply enchanting design. On the back of this pendant is a lovely quote from Jacques Cousteau: "The sea, once it casts its spell, holds one in its net of wonder forever."

MATERIALS

- 1 cast-pewter mermaid Green Girl Studios pendant
- 10 Hill Tribe silver stick beads
- 15 4mm acid green Czech glass faceted rondelles
- 15 4mm striated blue Czech glass faceted rondelles
- 1 sterling silver toggle clasp
- 4 5mm sterling silver jump rings
- 22-gauge sterling silver wire
- round-nose pliers
- 2 pairs chain-nose pliers
- wire cutters

Design Tip

Color inspiration can come from a theme, not from an image or object alone. In this case, I used colors that evoke the feeling of the ocean.

1

2

3

1 The core of this design is a wire-wrapped chain (see Making a Wrapped-Style Chain on page 24) alternating between green and blue beads. One segment is 16-beads long; another is 3-beads long, starting and ending with a green bead; the last segment is 11-beads long, starting and ending with a blue bead.

2 Begin to coil a 2" (5cm) wire segment. Slide it into the top bead on the 3-bead segment and finish as before. Thread on the silver stick beads. Begin to coil the end of the wire, thread it into the end of the 11-bead segment and finish as before.

3 Attach the 16-bead segment to the left side of the mermaid pendant with a jump ring (see opening and Closing Jump Rings on page 21). Attach the 3-bead-stick bead-11-bead segment to the right side of the mermaid pendant using a jump ring. Using the jump rings, attach the clasp to the open ends of the beaded sections.

Fashion forward

Firecracker

What is the same? I used the wire-wrapped chain method.

What is different? Small crystals make this chain even more delicate. Little wire accents dangle from the clasp to give it movement. I was thinking Fourth of July fireworks, and I think it worked out!

Layer Me Necklace

I love bright, vibrant colors. This necklace reminds me of Miami Beach. Because the colors are so intense, I kept the design simple. Three pretty yellow briolettes add a little movement and interest, and the hammered Quick Links work wonderfully with the frosted cat's eye glass and dyed agate beads.

Design Tip

Don't be afraid to use outrageous color combinations in your designs. The key is to make sure the colors are all the same saturation and shade. Had one of the beads been a pastel or a more translucent color in this design it wouldn't have had as much impact.

MATERIALS

- 68 4mm orange frosted cat's eye glass rondelles
- 26 dyed blue agate faceted ovals
- 59 4mm yellow frosted cat's eye glass rondelles
- 3 9mm × 14mm dyed yellow faceted agate briolettes
- 52-link section silver-plated rolo chain
- 49-strand .018 silver-colored Beadalon wire
- 3 ball-tipped silver-plated head pins
- 2 large textured solid silver-plated rings
- 1 large swivel lobster clasp
- 6 sterling silver EZ-Crimps
- 8 6mm silver-plated jump rings
- Mighty Crimp Tool
- round-nose pliers
- 2 pairs chain-nose pliers
- wire cutters

49

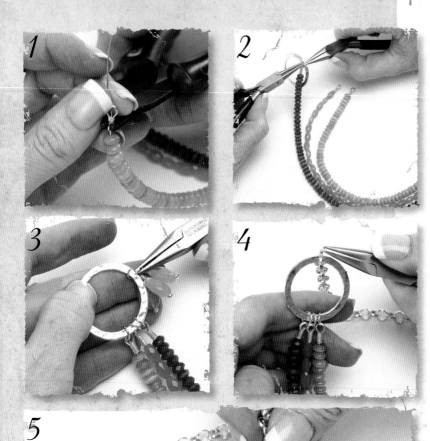

1 Attach an EZ-Crimp end to a 12" (30.5cm) segment of Beadalon wire (see Crimping Wire With an EZ-Crimp End on page 25). Slide on the orange beads and, while keeping the wire rounded, finish the other end with a second EZ-Crimp. Repeat for the blue beads and yellow beads.

2 Attach the beaded segments onto jump rings then onto one hammered link with the orange strand at the bottom, blue in the middle and yellow on top (see Opening and Closing Jump Rings on page 21). Repeat on the other end of each strand with a second hammered link.

3 Create wrapped dangles with the three agate briolettes and ball-tipped head pins (see Making a Wrapped Loop on page 15). Use a jump ring to attach them above the orange beaded strand on one of the hammered links.

4 Open a chain link to attach it to one of the hammered links (see Opening and Closing Chain Links on page 22).

5 Attach a lobster clasp to the other end of the chain. You will clasp the necklace on the large round link.

Fashion forward

Pretty Baby By Angela Bannatyne

What is the same? The basic style is the same: three strands connected to one.

What is different? The length is longer than the original piece. I used a vintage-inspired subdued color palette instead of the vibrant colors in the original design. The overall feel is more eclectic and less structured.

Flower Power Earrings

By wrapping the beads around the edges of these hammered frames, I created the look of wire and bead flowers. I usually wrap the beads flush to the front of the frames, but this was a happy accident. I love the tough and tender appeal of this design. The red, white and black color scheme is a longtime personal favorite.

Design Tip

If you don't like polishing metal, paint a coat of clear nail polish on your Quick Links to prevent them from tarnishing.

MATERIALS

10 5mm freshwater pearls

10 3mm jet AB CRYSTALLIZED-Swarovski Elements rounds

2 red AB CRYSTALLIZED-Swarovski Elements rounds

2 1" (2.5cm) Quick Links ovals

2 1" (2.5cm) Quick Links circles

2 dapped and coiled silver-plated ear wires

2 20-gauge sterling silver head pins

20-gauge silver-plated or sterling wire

2 6mm silver-plated jump rings

chasing hammer

steel bench block

round-nose pliers

2 pairs chain-nose pliers

wire cutters

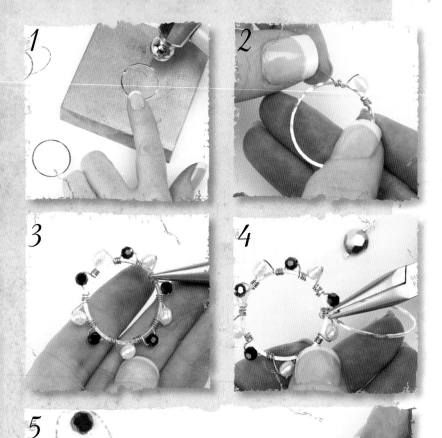

1 Place a Quick Link on the steel bench block (see Hammering Texture Into Wire and Metal on page 14). Use the round end of the hammer to texture one side of each link. Repeat for all the links.

2 Tightly wrap the wire around the circle frame three times (see Wire Wrapping Around a Base on page 16). Add a pearl and wrap the wire three more times. Alternate between pearls and jet beads until you reach the fifth jet bead.

3 After wrapping all the way around the, wrap the wire tail into the existing coil. Cut the excess wire with the wire cutters and use the needle-nose pliers to tuck the tail under.

4 Create coiled dangles with a red crystal and a head pin (see Making a Wrapped Loop on page 15). Attach the beaded circle to the hammered oval using a 6mm jump ring (see Opening and Closing Jump Rings on page 21).

5 Attach the ear wire and the beaded dangle to top of the hammered oval. Repeat steps 1-5 for the second earring.

Fashion forward

Blue Greens

What is the same? This is the same basic pattern.

What is different? I changed the color palette, used all CRYSTALLIZED-Swarovski elements and added a cube shape to the center of the wired dangle for more movement.

Psychedelia Bracelet

These striated beads in primary colors are so outrageously fantastic, they require little embellishment. A single matte onyx oval, some metal jump rings used as spacers, a small segment of gunmetal chain, a handcrafted clasp and three color-coordinated beaded dangles—and *voilà*! I'm a firm believer in the KISS school of design: Keep It Simple, Sweetie.

Design Tip

Annealed iron wire is very strong so rather than beat up my finer wire cutters, I opt for memory wire shears.

MATERIALS

4 20mm × 30mm flat rainbow calsilica ovals

18mm × 25mm flat matte onyx oval

10mm × 15mm vintage red German glass bow bead

8mm lime moonglow Lucite round

5mm × 10mm stabilized turquoise barrel bead

18-gauge annealed iron wire

4-link segment large gunmetal chain

2 sterling silver EZ-Crimp ends

3 star tip silver-plated head pins

24 6mm silver-plated jump rings

10mm silver-plated jump ring

pencil or dowel

memory wire shears

EZ-Crimp Tool

round-nose pliers

2 pairs chain-nose pliers

1 Attach an EZ-Crimp to one end of the wire (see Crimping Wire with an EZ-Crimp End on page 25). Thread a calsilica bead, 6 jump rings, an onyx bead, 6 jump rings, a calsilica bead, 6 jump rings, a calsilica bead, 6 jump rings and a final calsilica bead on the wire. Thread wire into a second EZ-Crimp and secure. Use wire cutters to clip off excess wire.

2 Create a simple wire hook using a 3" (7.5cm) segment of iron wire (see Making a Wire Hook on page 18). Thread three remaining beads on star head pins and create wrapped loop dangles (see Making a Wrapped Loop on page 15). Attach the hook and the beaded dangles to the EZ-Crimp on one end of the beaded section with a 5mm jump ring (see Opening and Closing Jump Rings on page 21).

3 Attach the 4-link chain segment to the EZ-Crimp on the opposite end of the beaded section, using a flat gunmetal chain link as the jump ring.

Fashion forward

Woodstock Summer
By Andrew Thornton

What is the same? Woodstock Summer *utilizes the same basic color scheme as Psychedelia: red, yellow and blue. These primary colors are punched up with black and silver accents. The movement of the dangles mimics the implied movement of the striated patterned beads.*

What is different? Breaking away from the simple approach, the dangles are reinvented and take center stage, providing movement and varied textures. The individual colors from Psychedelia are separated into dangles attached to large-linked chain that create new color combinations with the wearer's movement. This variation also mingles faceted, reflective and translucent materials with the opaque pieces to create interesting cast shadows and add a little sparkle.

Klee Necklace

This minimalist design is inspired by the work of artist Paul Klee. Matching saturated pastels with gunmetal is a surprisingly pleasant combination. This is all about "less is more." That's not to say that more can't sometimes be more, but I suggest that you err on the side of simplicity for designs that will always complement the wearer.

Design Tip

If you're feeling uninspired, a trip to an art museum might be just the ticket. Fine artists view the world through a fascinating and inspirational lens.

MATERIALS

4 Oriental Trading Company resin beads in oranges and yellows

1 Natural Touch aqua resin bead

1 lime tagua nut pendant

10-link section sterling silver open circle chain

12" (30.5cm) section large gunmetal chain

20-gauge anodized steel wire

5 10mm silver-plated jump rings

1 stamp with writing (I used Hero Arts Old Letter Writing Stamp S4878)

Ranger Archival Ink in jet black

round-nose pliers

2 pairs chain-nose pliers

memory wire shears

pencil or thin dowel

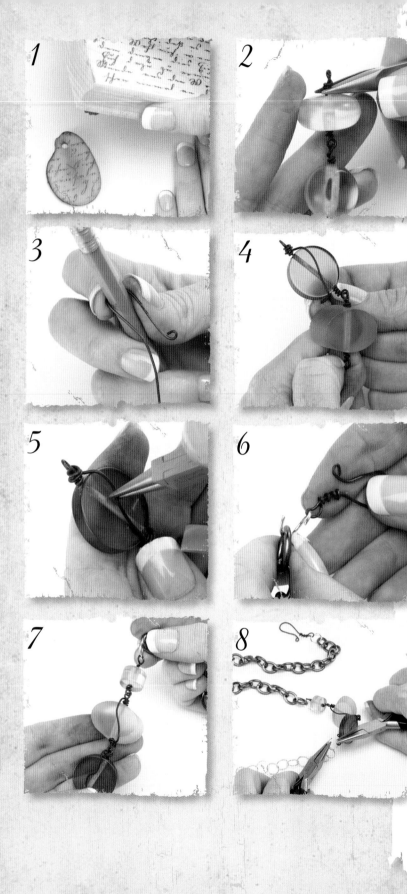

1 Remove the chain sections and set them aside (see Opening and Closing Chain Links on page 22). Stamp the tagua nut bead using archival ink and allow it to dry. You can opt to heat set the ink with a heat tool.

2 Thread a pink bead on a 4" (10cm) segment of wire and create a double organically wrapped loop (see Making a Wrapped-Style Chain on page 24). (Organic means the wires that create the wrap can be imperfect, giving the piece an organic feel.) Slip another 4" (10cm) segment of wire into one loop on the first bead, add a yellow rondelle and make a double-wrapped loop.

3 Use the wire, dowel, pliers and your fingers to create a large wrapped wire hook (see Making a Wrapped Wire Hook on page 19).

4 Thread an orange slice bead with a 4" (10cm) section of wire and create double loops. Add an aqua slice bead to the first bead as described in step 2. Wrap a 2" (5cm) section of wire around the coil on one of the beads, pull the wire across the bead and wrap the wire around the opposite side.

5 Use pliers or your fingers to gently shape wire into an S-shape. Repeat this process for the second slice bead, creating a slightly different shape with the wire.

6 Thread a pink rondelle on a 4" (10cm) segment of wire, and loop it into the aqua slice bead creating a double-wrapped loop. Attach the hook to one end of the gunmetal chain using a jump ring (see Opening and Closing Jump Rings on page 21).

7 Attach the 3-bead wire section to the opposite end with a jump ring.

8 Attach the sterling chain segment to the open end of the 3-bead section using a jump ring.

9

10

9 Attach the open end of the sterling chain segment to the 2-bead wire segment using a jump ring.

10 Attach another jump ring to the open end of the 2-bead segment. Attach the tagua nut slice with a jump ring to the bottom of the 2-bead section.

Fashion forward

Chained to Plexi By Tonia Davenport

What is the same? I used colored acrylic elements.

What is different? I choose to use a minimal amount of color, and a tiny bit of contrast for dramatic impact.

Chapter 3

Texture

Texture is a tricky design element. It can determine the overall mood of a piece of jewelry. That's why it's important to carefully consider what sorts of textures you're using and how to combine them effectively. Think about how different a smooth, high-polished silver bracelet is from a hammered, wire-decorated one. One feels chic and sophisticated, while the other feels bohemian and artsy. Now change that again by adding crystal or organically-shaped gemstones, and you'll see how much these elements can shift the mood of a design.

In this chapter, we'll play with subtle and extreme texture variations. We'll see what happens when we add or delete textural elements, and how doing so shapes the finished product. We'll play with interesting combinations of materials, taking some risks, and hopefully achieve pleasing results. You'll learn how to make a similar design unique merely by re-envisioning it with different elements.

Add to that what you've already learned about color and scale, and you'll begin to feel like a real jewelry designer. That's the idea! Keep up the good work!

"Texture is the most enduring and ubiquitous underpinning of form... certainly a calming, meditative and appealing world for both the eye and mind." Lynda Lehman

High Tea Bracelet

Here's to the ladies who lunch. Whip up this Victorian influenced charm bracelet, and you'll look like you belong at the country club, too. The textured gunmetal combined with a stark black-and-white color palette give this piece a vintage allure. A Green Girl Studios Moon Hare charm adds the perfect touch of whimsy.

MATERIALS

3 textured gunmetal filigree butterflies

1 Green Girl Studios pewter Moon Hare charm

4 10mm lava rock heart beads

4 8mm white agate beads

2 10mm × 15mm clear quartz ovals

1 15mm × 20mm black-and-white shell inlay striped oval bead

1 20mm × 12mm black onyx teardrop bead

20-gauge silver-plated German wire

14 ball tip silver-plated head pins

7" (18cm) section textured gunmetal chain

20 textured gunmetal chain links for jump rings

round-nose pliers

2 pairs chain-nose pliers

wire cutters

1 Remove chain segments and chain links using pliers (see Opening and Closing Chain Links on page 22). Create wrapped dangles for all beads on ball tip head pins (see Making a Wrapped Loop on page 15).

2 Create a wrapped wire hook (see Making a Wrapped Wire Hook on page 19). Add texture by squeezing the wire between the ends of the round-nose pliers.

3 Attach charms to the base chain using the 20 chain links as jump rings (see Opening and Closing Chain Links on page 22). Add the pewter charm to one end and the hook to the other. The first butterfly is added on the second link from the hook. On every other link, add the following: butterfly, white agate, lava, white agate, quartz, lava, inlay, butterfly, white agate, lava, quartz, onyx teardrop, white agate, lava, butterfly. There will be four open links on the charm end to allow for adjusting the bracelet when secured.

Fashion forward

Victoriana

What is the same? I kept the black-and-white palette and used many of the same beads.

What is different? The high-polished silver chain and lockets have changed the design entirely. It looks more modern and less vintage, but still has a sweet and romantic appeal. I also added some lovely and colorful lampworked beads. Mix up your metals and see what happens!

Strike It Bracelet

Oh how I adore simple, open geometric shapes repeated in a design! It's so mod and swingy! Add a dash of cool colors and funky shapes for accent, and you have a sassy, saucy little number to throw on your wrist. Hammering these shapes gives them a more rustic appearance.

Design Tip

If you opt to use plated metal like I did here, you may want to paint on a coating of clear nail polish to prevent it from tarnishing after you hammer it.

MATERIALS

3 10mm carnelian coin beads

3 5mm × 8mm reconstituted turquoise tubes

3 6mm green agate rounds

3 1" (2.5cm) silver-plated Quick Links circles

3 1" (2.5cm) silver-plated Quick Links ovals

3 ½" (1cm) silver-plated Quick Links circles

9 silver-plated head pins

5 silver-plated Quick Links connectors

1 large silver-plated swivel lobster clasp

7 6mm silver-plated jump rings

steel bench block

chasing hammer

round-nose pliers

2 pairs chain-nose pliers

wire cutters

1 Strike one side of each Quick Link with a chasing hammer on a steel block to create texture (see Hammering Texture into Wire and Metal on page 14). These little links are slippery; use your fingernail to secure them or double-sided tape that you can peel off after hammering.

2 Connect the larger links using Quick Link connectors, starting with an oval and a circle and alternating between the two until you reach the fourth circle.

3 Make wrapped beaded dangles using the head pins and one of each color of bead (see Making a Wrapped Loop on page 15). Attach a set of three dangles to the bottom of every large oval link with a jump ring (see Opening and Closing Jump Rings on page 21).

4 Attach a small hammered Quick Link to the bottom of every large circle link with a jump ring.

5 Attach the clasp to the large oval on the left side of the bracelet with a jump ring.

Fashion forward

Sunny Days

What is the same? I used the same pattern and the same links here.

What is different? I changed the colors, added more beads and added four open circles to each larger circle to give the design a lot more movement. I opted not to hammer the links, giving them a more mod feel.

Curlicue Earrings

One day after coiling wire around a jump ring maker tool, I pulled the coil off, gently tugged it apart and got these great little curlicues! They add just the right touch of whimsy to simple hammered copper earrings. You can take this idea so many places . . . what are you waiting for?

MATERIALS

20-gauge copper Artistic Wire

jump ring maker tool with ¼" (6mm) dowel

chasing hammer

steel bench block

sanding block

round-nose pliers

chain-nose pliers

wire cutters

1

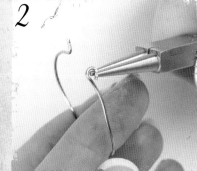

2

3

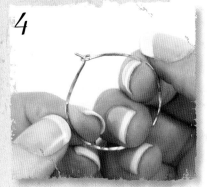

4

5

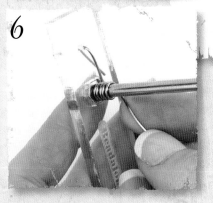

6

1 Cut off a 3" (7.5cm) segment of wire. Round it over the handle of the hammer to create a hoop shape.

2 Create a small loop at one end of the wire (see Turning a Loop on page 14). Bend the other end up at a 90-degree angle.

3 Place the ear wires on the steel bench block. Use the rounded end of the hammer to add texture to both sides of the ear wires (see Hammering Texture into Wire and Metal on page 14).

4 Adjust the shape of the wire hoops after hammering.

5 Using the sanding block, smooth the cut edge of the wire that goes into the ear.

6 Wrap the wire around a jump ring maker with a ¼" (6mm) dowel (See steps 1–5 of Making Jump Rings on page 20).

7 Remove the coil and gently pull it apart.

8 Cut off fourteen 3-coil segments using the wire cutters.

9 Use the round-nose pliers to make a small loop in one end and a larger loop in the opposite end. Make fourteen coils.

10 Thread the larger end of 7 looped wires on the earring. (Be sure the coils are all facing the same direction.) Repeat for second earring.

Design Tip
You can opt to secure the coils on the hoops using a crimp tube.

Fashion forward

Tendrils

What is the same? I used the same technique.

What is different? I used a thinner gauge of sterling silver wire. I added crystals to the ends of each wire before turning the loops. I didn't do any hammering so these have a shinier appearance. I hung three longer and leaner coils from each French ear wire for a more linear design.

Blackbeard's Bounty Necklace

A tangled mass of gunmetal and black chains is accented with a judicious sprinkling of black crystal pearls. I'm simply mad for this design; it's one that makes you want to dive in deep and savor every lovely layer. The surprise here is a pewter Green Girl Studios skeleton key charm that dangles secretly down your back. This is deliciously decadent, *n'est-ce pas?*

Design Tip

This design works best with a wide variety of chains.

MATERIALS

14 8mm black CRYSTALLIZED-Swarovski Elements crystal pearls

1 lava rock heart bead

1 Green Girl Studios skeleton key charm

10 16" (41cm) segments, varied size and shapes of gunmetal and black chain

1 8-link segment large and small oval gunmetal chain

1 silver-plated large spring ring clasp

14 gunmetal head pins

2 silver-plated head pins

1 black chain link used as jump ring

2 10mm silver-plated jump rings

round-nose pliers

2 pairs chain-nose pliers

wire cutters

1 Remove 10 various 16" (41cm) lengths of gunmetal and black chain using two pairs of chain-nose pliers (see Opening and Closing Chain Links on page 22). Make pearl dangles and one lava rock bead dangle using gunmetal head pins (see Making a Wrapped Loop on page 15). Attach 13 of the pearl dangles to the smaller links in a 16" (41cm) section of large and small oval gunmetal chain.

2 Attach the last link in each chain to the 10mm jump ring and one end of the clasp (see Opening and Closing Jump Rings on page 21). Repeat for the opposite sides.

3 Attach the key, the remaining pearl and the heart to the end of the 8-link chain segment.

4 Attach the opposite end to the 10mm jump ring on one end of the necklace. Attach clasp.

Design Tip

Use heavy-duty jump rings for this project.

Fashion forward

Copper-nicus By Rebecca Peck

What is the same? I loved Margot's design and decided to go with multiple strands for mine as well.

What is different? I added a little more color to my design and used several different types of beads to achieve texture.

Dark Night of the Soul Necklace

Stunning vintage copper leaves inspired this moody, textured design. I used mottled jasper beads, gray polyester and gunmetal chains and findings. This design would have an entirely different appeal if you used copper or sterling silver. This is absolutely gorgeous around the neck, which is where it belongs on your more introspective days.

MATERIALS

7 1¾" (4.5cm) vintage copper etched leaves

10 8mm faceted fancy jasper coin beads

5½" (14cm) section gray polyester chain

10½" (27cm) segment short– and long–link gunmetal chain

11" (28cm) segment dapped, fine short– and long–link gunmetal chain

10 gunmetal head pins

1 gunmetal toggle clasp set

1 gunmetal toggle circle

3 gunmetal chain links used as jump rings

10 5mm gunmetal jump rings

round-nose pliers

2 pairs chain-nose pliers

wire cutters

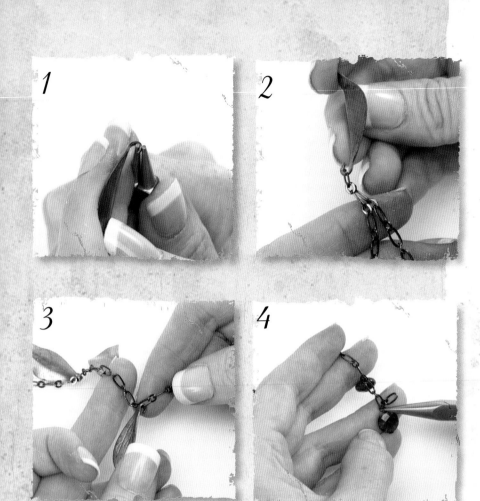

1 The leaves I used didn't have a bail, so I took round-nose pliers and bent the stem back and over to create one. (You could opt for some regular copper leaf pendants to mimic this look.)

2 Thread a leaf into the center of the smaller chain. Use the chain-nose pliers to squeeze the loop shut to secure the leaf to the chain.

3 Moving two large links over, attach a leaf on the third large link on each side of the center. Repeat, adding a leaf on every third link for a total of 7 leaves.

4 Create looped dangles using gunmetal head pins and the coin beads (see Turning a Loop on page 14). Attach them to each third chain link, starting with the third from the outermost leaf on each side of the necklace.

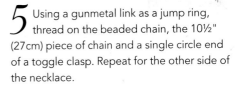

5 Using a gunmetal link as a jump ring, thread on the beaded chain, the 10½" (27cm) piece of chain and a single circle end of a toggle clasp. Repeat for the other side of the necklace.

6 Attach the polyester chain to one of the toggle circles with a gunmetal jump ring.

7 Attach the bar end of a toggle clasp to the other end of the polyester chain using the gunmetal jump ring.

Amber Evenings By Tammy Powley

What is the same? The basic theme of the design is the same, in that it includes a double-strand necklace with seven leaves as the focal points. The earthtone color palette is also similar.

What is different? To play with the idea of texture, I included glass leaves (from glass artist D.D. Hess) versus copper leaves. Rather than use chain alone for the necklace straps, I added some fiber in the form of waxed linen cord for one of the necklace strands. Rather than having faceted jasper beads dangling from the chain, I stationed smoky quartz colored crystals a few inches apart to connect pieces of chain for the inside strand. I also included a little bit of green to create a color contrast in the center of the necklace.

71

Dzi Dreams Necklace

This is a darker and more pensive design than my usual Technicolor palette. What can I say? I'm a girl of many moods. I love the smooth symmetrical beads alongside the more organic shapes, and the touch of textured metal adds a little excitement to the mix. Real Tibetan Dzi beads are extremely rare and some people consider them powerfully magical. These are reproductions, but when you wear this design you'll feel pretty magical, too.

Design Tip

Use a multichannel bead board so you can be sure your multistrand designs nestle into one another beautifully. I also recommend testing the design on a neck form (or yourself) before you commit the final crimp to make any small adjustments.

MATERIALS

42 6mm jade nuggets

23 6mm faceted tiger's eye coins

22 10mm striped agate beads

6 faux Dzi agate beads

9 17mm × 20mm onyx twisted oval beads

19- or 49-strand .018 silver-colored Beadalon wire

6 sterling silver EZ-Crimp ends

3 textured Bali sterling silver spacers

1 silver-plated triple strand slide clasp

6 6mm silver-plated jump rings

EZ-Crimp Tool

wire cutters

bead board

1. Arrange the beads on the bead board before stringing them. The top channel should have approximately 42 jade nuggets (adjust for your neck size). The next channel should have 23 tiger's eye coin beads alternating with 22 striped agate rounds. The bottom channel from left to right has 8 twisted onyx, Dzi, sterling silver spacer, Dzi, onyx, Dzi, sterling silver spacer, Dzi, sterling silver spacer and a final Dzi.

2. Attach the wire to an EZ-Crimp end (see Crimping Wire with an EZ-Crimp End on page 25). Connect it with a jump ring to an outer connector on one side of the secured clasp and bead the top strand of jade.

3. Attach the wire to the other side of the secured clasp, as in step 2. The wires need to be on the same outer link on each side. Before you crimp, test it on a neck form (or yourself) to ensure the proper fit.

4. Bead the next two strands with the longest strand attached to the bottom loop on the back of the clasp on each side and the middle strand attached to the middle loops on each side of the clasp.

5. Crimp each strand, but only do the first step of crimping to allow room for movement between the beads. This will protect the wire and make the design more fluid when worn.

Fashion forward

Sweet Cream By Jean Yates

What is the same? This is a similar pattern done in a bracelet focusing on the outside stringing.

What is different? I used different materials and a lighter color palette. The crystal and dichroic glass combined with the soft color of rose quartz make the design light and feminine. I altered the pattern by using different materials in a different configuration.

Chapter 4

Pattern

Everything in the material world is comprised of mathematical equations. When and image is broken down via computer programs, something called fractal images are created that are exquisitely beautiful and intricate works of patterned art. Art is math and math is art. Yes, there's math in art.

Pattern can be repetitive or it can be asymmetrical or it can seem entirely random, but even random things have a pattern and an order of their own. When you design, it's important to consider the patterns you are creating. You'll be surprised how changing one element in a pattern will impact the finished design.

In this chapter, we'll make patterns and then we'll remake them with slight or sweeping changes. We'll add and delete materials to see what happens. We'll explore order and dive into disorder and hopefully emerge with a deeper understanding of the design process.

You can find patterns for inspiration virtually everywhere you go, in fabrics and magazine ads and random piles of similar objects. Once you start to see patterns, you will spot them everywhere. Then you can mine those patterns for your designs.

"A repeated shape is not actually the same—the more subtle, the more poetic this repeat is, the more we feel that resonant pulse." Suzanne Northcott

Flower Chain Bracelet

Chain maille has been a trend for a few years now, and although I'm not blessed with the patience required to weave metal masterpieces from tiny jump rings, I do love to play with the techniques. This bracelet uses silver-plated rings in various sizes and features a simple flower chain core. I'm a big fan of silver, straight up and shiny.

MATERIALS

12 15mm silver-plated textured rings

10 10mm silver-plated Quick Links circles

1 silver-plated 3-strand slide clasp

51 10mm silver-plated jump rings

46 6mm silver-plated jump rings

2 pairs chain-nose pliers

Combustible

What is the same? I created a flower chain with 5mm copper jump rings.

What is different? I added beaded jump rings on either side of the single links on the chain with white heart African trade beads. I freeform wrapped a gorgeous Venetian Glass bead in wire as a focal and created my own hook clasp.

1 Begin with the core strand. Attach 2 5mm jump rings to the center connector on a 3-strand clasp.

2 To create a flower chain, alternate single and triple jump ring segments. The triple jump ring segments are threaded into each other to form a flower as shown.

3 Add a flower, a 5mm jump ring, a single ring, a 5mm jump ring and a flower alternating between them in this established pattern until you have 12 flowers and 11 single rings.

4 Attach the final flower to the center connector on the opposite side of the 3-strand clasp with two jump rings. This is the core section, and you'll be building on each side of it. Begin on one side by attaching a textured ring to an outside connector on the clasp with a 10mm jump ring.

5 Alternate between textured rings and the Quick Links circles using 5mm jump rings to connect them.
When you reach the sixth textured ring, attach it to the coordinating connector on the opposite side of the clasp with a 10mm jump ring. Repeat for the opposite side.

6 To connect the interior and exterior segments, use 5mm jump rings on each exterior link attached to the 10mm jump rings on the interior segment as shown. This is almost like weaving a fabric segment. Check all of the rings to make sure they're secure.

Design Tip

You can take a technique and get a different result by changing the scale or the kinds of materials you use. Explore, experiment and enjoy!

Effortless Elegance Earrings

There could be nothing simpler than these bent wire earrings with beaded dangles, and yet they're fascinating. It's easy to make your own ear wires, and you can endlessly play with scale and shape and embellishments. I'm mad for these, and plan to make them in a rainbow of colors!

MATERIALS

2 12mm × 17mm black onyx polished teardrop beads

6 3mm red coral beads

6 24-gauge sterling silver head pins

2 ball tip sterling silver head pins

20-gauge sterling silver wire

thin metal dowel (I used the metal end of a rattail comb)

sanding block

round-nose pliers

chain-nose pliers

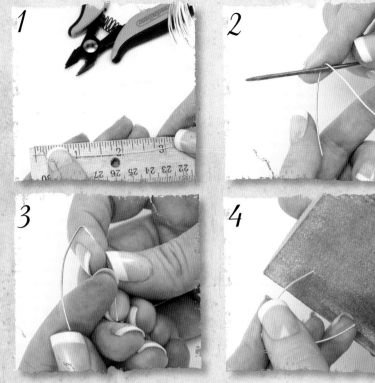

1
2

3

4

5

6

1 Cut off two 3" (7.5cm) segments of wire.

2 Bend each wire segment over the thin dowel to create a crease or point not quite in the center of the wire, and in the same spot on both wires.

3 Gently round both wire tails into a matching curve.

4 Using the sanding block, sand the ends of the wire.

5 Bend a loop in one end of wire using the round-nose pliers.

6 Create wrapped dangles using ball tip head pins and onyx beads (see Making a Wrapped Loop on page 15). Repeat for the coral beads using regular head pins. Using the chain-nose pliers to open and close the loop at the end of each ear wire, attach the beads to the loop, onyx dangle first followed by the three coral dangles.

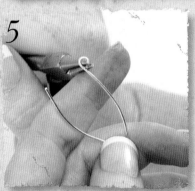

Fashion forward

Citrus

What is the same? I made similar ear wires and added dangles.

What is different? I hammered the front half of the ear wires to add texture. I attached a hammered oval Quick Link, which I wire wrapped with three olivine crystals and dangled a mint colored stone tablet bead from each hoop. The simple design rose to a whole new level with just a few adjustments.

79

Oh So Coco Necklace

Coco Chanel is one of my icons. I used to have a shrine to her above my bed because she is "The Goddess of Fashion." Coco understood that every woman wants to shine, and she made clothing that freed women while allowing them to be uniquely fabulous. Her love of pearls and chains inspired this design. You could opt to put a pretty faux flower in place of the bow. This brushed metal chain is really sumptuous, and I love it paired with the rosary-style pearls.

Design Tip

Look to the masters for great jewelry ideas, and always be sure to give credit where it is due. Be inspired and make it your own!

MATERIALS

39 8mm faux pearls

1 Blue Moon Beads Noir Fleur de Lis connector

12½" (32cm) segment Noir matte black chain

15" (38cm) segment Noir matte black chain

1 Noir matte black toggle clasp

6 4mm gunmetal jump rings

39 gunmetal head pins

1" (2.5cm) wide organza ribbon with silver thread detail

Aleene's Stop Fraying (optional)

round-nose pliers

2 pairs chain-nose pliers

wire cutters

ruler

1 Measure and cut the chain segments (see Opening and Closing Chain Links on page 22). Create the rosary chains with the pearls (see Creating a Rosary-Style Chain on page 23); there is one 10-pearl segment and one 29-pearl segment.

2 Attach the shorter pearl chain to the top of the fleur de lis connector with a jump ring (see Opening and Closing Jump Rings on page 21).

3 Attach the circle end of the toggle clasp to the other end of the shorter pearl chain.

4 Thread the other chains onto the bottom of the fleur de lis using jump rings with the longest chain at the bottom, the 29-pearl chain in the middle and the shorter chain on top.

5 Connect them to the bar end of the toggle clasp using 2 links removed from the chain (see Opening and Closing Chain Links on page 22).

6 Tie a bow around the jump ring at the top of the fleur de lis connection. You can either let the ends fray or dab the ends of the bow with Stop Fraying or other fabric-friendly clear drying glue.

Jet

Fashion forward

What is the same? I used a similar overall pattern and measurements.

What is different? I replaced the pearls with CRYSTALLIZED-Swarovski Elements 8mm rounds in padparadscha, black diamond and Indian sapphire for a more colorful palette. The bow here is black satin, which I'm allowing to fray for a distressed look.

81

Crazy Lace Bracelet

Keishi pearls are enchantingly beautiful with their organic shapes and lustrous sheen. This bracelet features a simple double-needle ladder stitch with a varied number of round and keishi pearls on each side for an asymmetrical appeal. This idea can be implemented in a variety of ways—use beads of the same size and shape to get a completely different effect. Mix up sizes and shapes and see what happens.

Design Tip

Even the most basic of bead stitches becomes interesting when you play with the pattern. The worst thing that can happen is that it doesn't work, but you'll learn something in the process. Never be afraid to make glorious mistakes.

MATERIALS

43 3mm cream freshwater pearls

27 4mm cream keishi pearls

62 TB-21F silver-lined clear Toho Aiko seed beads

49-strand .015 Beadalon wire

4 sterling silver EZ-Crimp ends

1 large sterling silver swivel lobster clasp

Mighty Crimp Tool

2 6mm silver-plated jump rings

2 pairs chain-nose pliers

wire cutters

Tacky Mat, bead board or bead cloth

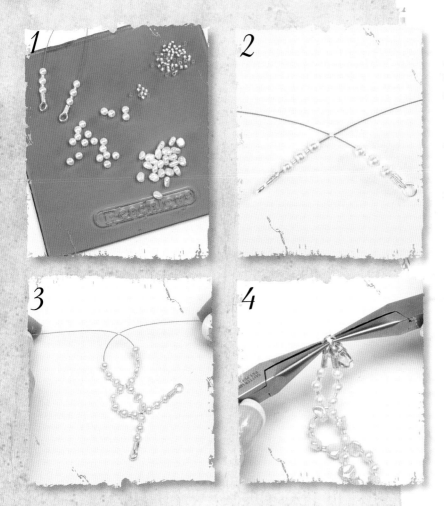

1 Place the beads on a Tacky Mat, bead board or bead cloth. Attach EZ-Crimp ends to two 12" (30.5cm) strands of wire. Slide a round pearl, seed bead, round pearl, seed bead and a round pearl on each wire.

2 Thread both wires into opposite sides of a seed bead.

3 You will be beading both wires and threading them into seed beads to create this pattern as you move along. The pattern I've used is as follows:

Left wire: keishi pearl (KP), seed bead, KP, seed bead, 1 pearl (P), seed bead (thread in), P, 2KP, P, seed bead, KP, 2P, seed bead (thread in), P, 2KP, P, KP, seed bead (thread in), 3KP, seed bead, KP, P, KP, P, seed bead (thread in), KP, 2P, KP, seed bead, P, KP, P, seed bead (thread in), 3KP.

Right wire: 3P, KP, P, seed bead (thread in), 3P seed bead, 2P, 2KP, seed bead (thread in), P, KP, P, seed bead (thread in), 3P, KP, seed bead (thread in), 3P, seed bead (thread in), 2KP, P, seed bead (thread in), 4KP, seed bead (thread in), 3P.

4 Thread the wires into the EZ-Crimps and finish. Clip off the excess wire. Attach a jump ring on both ends of the bracelet, adding the lobster clasp to one side.

Hot and Spicy

What is the same? I used the double-needle ladder stitch.

What is different? This design is symmetrical and the colors are vibrant. The CRYSTALLIZED-Swarovski Elements beads give it a beautiful sparkle and a more elegant appearance.

Wild Waves Necklace

Four strands of exposed and beaded white wire weave in and out of one another creating a mesmerizing wave pattern. This gorgeous necklace has a summertime palette that works beautifully with a crisp white shirt or your everyday denim. Change the colors to suit your taste.

Design Tip

This architecturally inspired design uses tension to suspend the beads along the wire. If you use different beads you may have to change the wire diameter. Continually adjust the tension as you bead; it will help give the finished piece the right amount of structure.

MATERIALS

17 8mm Indian sapphire CRYSTALLIZED-Swarovski Elements rounds

17 8mm white alabaster CRYSTALLIZED-Swarovski Elements rounds

16 6mm crystal AB CRYSTALLIZED-Swarovski Elements briolette-cut rondelles

112 4mm Indian red CRYSTALLIZED-Swarovski Elements bicones

Beadalon 7-strand .018 white wire

8 sterling silver EZ-Crimp ends

1 large silver-plated swivel lobster clasp

4 6mm silver-plated jump rings

Mighty Crimp Tool

2 pairs chain-nose pliers

wire cutters

1

Cut off four 21" (53cm) sections of white wire. Attach EZ-Crimp ends to two of the strands (see Crimping Wire with an EZ-Crimp End on page 25). Create the core of the design by threading an Indian sapphire bead on one strand and a white alabaster bead on the other. Thread both strands into a crystal AB rondelle.

2

Continue this pattern until you reach the final Indian sapphire/white alabaster section. Attach EZ-Crimp ends to each wire.

3

Attach EZ-Crimp ends to the remaining two wires. Using one of the newly-crimped wires, attach it to the core beaded strands with a jump ring (see Opening and Closing Jump Rings on page 21).

Slide 7 Indian red bicones onto the wire. Thread the wire between the beads coming from above the core wires, right behind the first white rondelle (only bare wire will go between the wires). Bead the Indian red strand with 7 more beads, and repeat threading though the core wires just after the next white rondelle, alternating the direction as you go.

4

Continue the wave pattern until you reach the final Indian sapphire/white alabaster section Secure the wire with an EZ-Crimp end. Cut off any excess wire.

5

With the remaining crimped wire, add it to the jump ring at the beginning of the necklace. Weave this bare wire through the openings of the core wire as desired. When you reach the end, secure the wire with an EZ-Crimp.

6

Secure all the EZ-Crimps with jump rings, arranging the wires so the pattern remains solidified at both ends. Attach a second jump ring to the open end. Attach a swivel lobster clasp to one end.

Rivenrock By Jean Campbell

What is the same? The general technique is the same—we both wove multiple wires and beads into a strand. The tension of the beads on the wire holds the pieces together.

What is different? Margot's Wild Waves design employs the wire to give the illusion that there is a wave of crystals going throughout the necklace. In Rivenrock, the pattern is interrupted with silver bicones, creating definite bundles of beads. The beads used produce a definite difference: Margot's are bright and luminous; mine are earthy and opaque.

Sticks and Stones Necklace

Carnelian is one of my favorite stones. I love the translucent nature of the material and the warmth of the color. This necklace is a study in simplicity with a lovely array of carnelian stick beads and one iridescent black cube nestled among the bunch. Brown leather gives a rustic feel, and a peace symbol on the back adds just the right Summer-of-Love accent. It's a less-is-more idea, because jewelry should enhance your beauty, not detract from it.

MATERIALS

22 polished carnelian round stick beads

1 15mm square iridescent black pillow bead

1 cast-pewter peace sign pendant

8" (20cm) segment .018 19- or 49-strand Beadalon wire

2 8½" (21.5cm) segments 1mm black leather cord

20-gauge annealed iron wire

2 sterling silver EZ-Crimp ends

1 5mm gunmetal jump ring

jeweler's glue

pencil or dowel

memory wire shears

EZ-Crimp Tool

round-nose pliers

2 pairs chain-nose pliers

wire cutters

1

1 Attach an EZ-Crimp to one end of the wire (see Crimping Wire With an EZ-Crimp End on page 25). Thread 7 carnelian sticks in various colors and sizes on the wire. Thread the pillow bead onto the wire.

2

2 Thread the remaining carnelian sticks on the wire. Attach a second EZ-Crimp to the open end of the wire. Round the wire before crimping, to allow for movement and prevent the design from being too stiff. Use wire cutters to remove the excess wire.

3

3 Make a wrapped hook using approximately 2" (5cm) of annealed iron wire (see Making a Wrapped Wire Hook on page 19).

To make the eye of the clasp: Using the annealed iron wire, wrap the first ½" (1cm) of the wire around the jaws of the round-nose pliers.

4

4 Using the memory wire shears, cut the wire ½" (1cm) from the first loop. Repeat the loop on the other end of the wire to make a tight S-shape. The loops should be the same size. Use chain-nose pliers to make adjustments.

5

5 Knot one leather strand to each of the EZ-Crimps.

6

6 Knot one strand into the eye you created in steps 3–4. Knot the other strand to the hook. Add the peace sign pendant on a jump ring to the eye of the hook end.

Use the jeweler's glue to secure the knots. Allow it to dry overnight before wearing.

Fashion forward

Copper Tone By Tammy Powley

What is the same? I kept to an earthtone palette, and many of the bead shapes such as the stick beads and square glass beads. I also included carnelian beads. I left part of the beading wire showing, just as the leather strap is exposed in the original design. The length is the same and is designed to hit near the collarbone.

What is different? The carnelian stick beads inspired me to create my own stick beads using copper metal clay. After polishing them, I textured them with a hammer. My carnelian beads are a different shape, and though I have a few square beads, mine are amber in color versus black. I also felt the need to organize the beads into a symmetrical pattern.

Chapter 5

Foundations

A good foundation is the key to success in anything you build. Using the wrong size wire or a chain that is too delicate are the main reasons designs fall apart. Even seasoned designers sometimes fall prey to the wrong combination of materials. Changing the structure of what lies beneath your beads will have a huge impact on the finished design. Leather has a totally different feel from chain or wire, for instance.

In this chapter, we'll explore what happens when you create a similar design using different foundations. We'll play with memory wire, leather, chain and hard and soft wire, and we'll explore how they inform the finished piece. We'll consider what foundation will best serve our ideas and explore the options in our work.

A good design is the sum of its parts, and a good designer understands intuitively what foundation will best serve her ideas. Jewelry making requires trial and error; that is, the testing of your materials to see what they can withstand. You can alter the appearance and the structure of a design by changing the element underneath; and I'll show you how!

"Do not worry if you have built your castles in the air. They are where they should be. Now put the foundations under them." Henry David Thoreau

Wrap and Hammer Earrings

Take a plain pair of wire hoops and hammer them. Then add a sprinkling of gemstones and crystals and, *voilà*! Instant artisan glamour!

MATERIALS

2 6mm violet Czech glass rondelles

2 4mm crystal AB Czech glass rondelles

2 4mm jonquil CRYSTALLIZED-Swarovski Elements bicones

24-gauge sterling silver wire

2 1" (2.5cm) sterling silver wire hoop earrings

chasing hammer

steel bench block

wire cutters

1

2

3

4

5

1 Use the round end of a chasing hammer and the steel bench block to gently texture the hoops (see Hammering Texture into Wire and Metal on page 14). Use your fingers to reshape the hoops after hammering.

2 Working on one hoop at a time, wrap wire three times around the lower half of the hoop (see Wrapping Wire Around a Base on page 16). Add a jonquil crystal and wire it onto the front of the hoop.

3 Wrap the wire three more times, and add on a crystal AB rondelle. Wire the rondelle onto the top front of the hoop.

4 Wrap the wire twice more and add the violet rondelle. Wire it onto the bottom front of the hoop, bending it sideways as shown.

5 Move up ⅛" (3mm) and wrap the wire tightly around the hoop three times. Clip off the excess wire and tuck the tail under with pliers. Repeat steps 2–3 for the second earring in a mirror image so you have a left and a right finished earring.

Fashion forward

Sizzle Hoops

What is the same? I used a similar wire-wrapped idea.

What is different? I used a prehammered Quick Links circle and added much more wire. The hoop here is flat, so the wire becomes far more important to the overall design. I wrapped the briolette behind the frame so it peeks out of the bottom. The colors are much more intense, and I've hung the hook from an ear wire to create a swingier style.

The Grid Necklace

This open-grid pendant seemed to beg for a simple wire-wrapping, so how could I refuse? I also wrapped the stainless steel choker with wire and crystals. The combined effect has a thoroughly mod vibe. I left half of the pendant open, but fill it up if you prefer.

Design Tip

Wire wrapping is all about tension. Take your time and wrap the wire tightly to ensure the best results. Don't be discouraged if it's not perfect at first—it takes practice. Besides, perfect lacks character. It helps to continually smooth the wire as you're wrapping to keep it malleable and kink-free.

MATERIALS

2" (5cm) open-grid sterling silver pendant

2 6mm padparadscha CRYSTALLIZED-Swarovski Elements rounds

9 6mm Indian red CRYSTALLIZED-Swarovski Elements rounds

10 6mm Indian sapphire CRYSTALLIZED-Swarovski Elements rounds

9 6mm light topaz CRYSTALLIZED-Swarovski Elements rounds

16" (41cm) stainless steel choker form

22-gauge German-style wire

10mm silver-plated jump ring

2 pairs chain-nose pliers

wire cutters

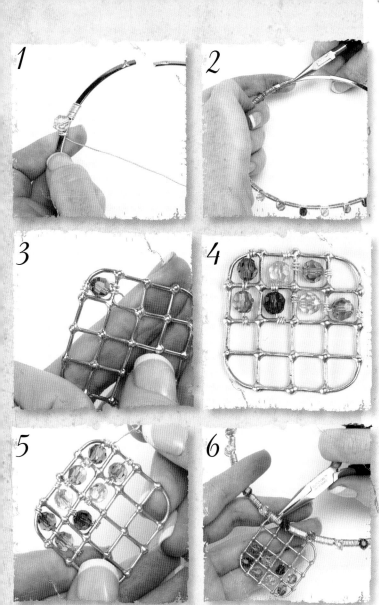

1 Cut off a length of the 22-gauge wire with which you can easily work. Starting 2½" (6cm) down from the clasp mechanism, tightly wrap the wire around the base 11 times, moving down with each wrap (see Wrapping Wire Around a Base on page 16). The idea is to keep the wire as tightly coiled and snug as you can without having it overlap. (If you run out of wire, patch more in using the chain-nose pliers to tuck the tail into the back of the base.) Add an Indian sapphire bead and wrap it to the front of the base. Then create 11 more wraps.

2 Add beads on in the following pattern: Indian sapphire, Indian red, light topaz. Continue alternating beads until you reach the final light topaz bead on the opposite side. Use wire cutters to clip excess wire and a pair of chain-nose pliers to tuck the tails under the base.

3 To embellish the grid, start by wrapping a wire three times around the frame of an outer edge. Thread on an Indian red crystal and wrap the wire tightly three times around the bar on the opposite bar of the opening.

4 Move over one space and repeat the process using an Indian sapphire crystal. Move down one space beneath the sapphire bead and wrap a light topaz bead into the open space. Repeat for the space beneath the Indian red bead. The next four-square grid is wired at a 90-degree angle from the first, as shown.

5 Substitute one padparadscha crystal for one of the Indian sapphire crystals in this four-square grid. Tuck wire tails under carefully with the chain-nose pliers.

6 Attach the grid pendant to the center of the necklace using a jump ring (see Opening and Closing Jump Rings on page 21).

Keyhole Grid By Melanie Brooks

What is the same? The centerpiece was inspired by the grid concept; the wired beads form a square structure. I also wire-wrapped crystal beads onto a neck wire form.

What is different? I changed the metal color from all silver to brass. The colored beads are exchanged for clear and almost colorless varieties. I built a grid around a focal piece, instead of building onto the grid.

Moody Blues Necklace

Memory wire is far more versatile than most folks realize. In this case, small segments of beaded memory wire create structure for the large rosary-style beads in a stunningly chic design. It's always fun to explore alternative materials in your work. You never know what you might discover when you ask the question, "What if?" The color palette here is soothing and vintage-inspired and this piece is overflowing with interesting textures.

MATERIALS

3 4-bead segments of 20mm Blue Moon Beads acrylic bead rosary-style chain

20 gray mother of pearl shell tusk beads

15 6mm aquamarine rounds

1 12mm × 20mm black onyx teardrop

1 Plaid Fresh open center floral silhouette pendant

1 10-link segment gunmetal curb chain

1 silver-plated hummingbird and flower toggle clasp

4 silver-plated or gunmetal head pins

3 2¼" (6cm) segments memory wire

2 oval chain links

memory wire shears

round-nose pliers

2 pairs chain-nose pliers

wire cutters

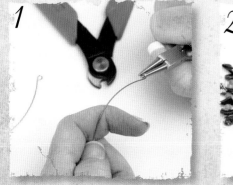

1. Cut the memory wire lengths using the memory wire shears. Turn one end of each memory wire with round-nose pliers (see Turning a Loop on page 14). The loop should curve toward the arc of the wire.

2. Fill each wire segment with mother of pearl and aqua marine beads; the number of beads will vary based on the selection. I used a random smattering of beads but you can opt for a pattern if you prefer. When you have finished filling each wire, turn a loop to close the beaded section.

3. Connect the 4-bead rosary sections and the memory wire sections, linking them with the outside loop on the final bead in each rosary chain. The pattern from left to right is: rosary chain, memory wire segment, rosary chain, memory wire segment, rosary chain, memory wire segment.

4. Attach the clasp. The circle end attaches to the final memory wire segment on the right side. Use two oval chain links to attach the bar end of the clasp to the end of the left side of the design (see Opening and Closing Chain Links on page 22).

5. Created wrapped dangles for the remaining aqua marine beads (see Making a Wrapped Loop on page 15). Create a looped dangle with the onyx teardrop. Thread the curb chain segment through the pendant and over the center section of the necklace, connecting the end links into a circle so it forms a bail.

Design Tip

Never cut memory wire with regular cutters or you'll ruin them. Always use memory wire shears.

6 Attach the onyx teardrop to the center of the chain so it hangs in the center of the pendant.

7 Attach the aqua marine dangle to the chain link above the teardrop using a gunmetal jump ring.

Butterfly Dusk By Jean Yates

What is the same? I used the same focal pendant concept with metal mesh attaching it to the core wire.

What is different? I chose a more feminine inspired palette with shades of purple and pink and whimsical design elements for a Victorian-style aesthetic. Instead of memory wire segments, I used a beaded-chain foundation.

Talisman Bracelet

Beautiful cast charms from the folks at Green Girl Studios inspired this magical gathering of talismans, vintage buttons, pearls, Austrian crystals and a single African trade bead drifting organically between knotted strands of leather. A steampunk themed Earthenwood Studio bead serves as a striking button for a rough-hewn clasp. This came together without much help from me; that is, I find designs like this to be like moving meditations. I just follow my intuition and see where it leads. In this case, it led me someplace quite surprising.

MATERIALS

- 4 vintage buttons
- 15mm hammered metal disc
- 1 African trade bead
- 1 tiny mermaid baby charm
- 1 owl charm
- 1 metal swirl charm
- 1 Hill Tribe silver star
- 1 black dice bead
- 1 steampunk center hole bead
- 1 2-hole drilled rock bead
- 1 4mm smoky quartz CRYSTALLIZED-Swarovski Elements bicone
- 1 4mm light smoked topaz CRYSTALLIZED-Swarovski Elements round
- 1 4mm cream freshwater pearl
- 1 3mm cream freshwater pearl
- 1 2mm carnelian round
- 1 8mm smoky quartz faceted coin bead
- 1 4mm faceted turquoise Czech oval
- 1 10mm × 18mm celadon green flat rectangle bead
- 1½mm black leather cord or other knot-friendly stringing material
- 22-gauge silver-plated ColourCraft wire
- 8 6mm silver-plated jump rings
- 4 10mm silver-plated jump rings
- Fabri-Tac (or other porous material friendly glue)
- round-nose pliers
- 2 pairs chain-nose pliers
- wire cutters

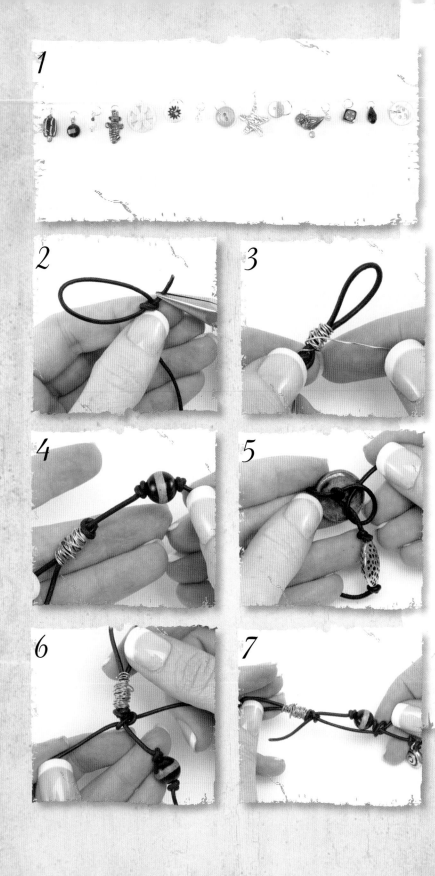

1 Select a variety of charms and beads for your creation. Add jump rings to the items that don't already have them (see Opening and Closing Jump Rings on page 21).

2 Cut two 10" (25.5cm) lengths of thin leather or other knot-friendly stringing material. Begin by creating the looped side of the closure. Knot one strand of leather leaving a 2" (5cm) loop. Use the chain-nose pliers to help pull the knot tight.

3 Wrap wire around the loop, leaving enough space for the button or clasp to slide through and remain secure when worn. Trim the excess wire with the wire cutters.

4 Move down about 1" (2.5cm) from the loop and knot the leather. Slide on a bead. Knot the leather flush to the end of the bead.

5 Repeat sliding on the beads every 1" (2.5cm) and knotting the leather until you reach the final bead. Thread the leather through the button clasp and around, and knot it flush to the back base of the clasp.

6 Knot a second strand of leather onto the base of the loop on the first strand.

7 Knot this second strand at the base of each bead as shown.

8 Finish by knotting the second strand onto the end of the first, behind the button clasp.

9 Secure the knots with glue and allow them to cure overnight. Cut off any excess leather after the glue cures.

10 Use 2 pairs of chain-nose pliers to add the various charms and dangles (created in step 1) onto the leather in between the base beads.

Cascabeleo By Jennifer Heynen

What is the same? I kept the foundation the same; I really liked the knotted leather in the Talisman Bracelet. I also included the charm elements.

What is different? Since I mostly work in bright colors, I felt inclined to include them in my necklace. That's why I included the ceramic beads, the glass beads and the seed beads. Multiple layers in the necklace provide for another element of fun.

Nights in Tunisia Necklace

The vivid blue-coated chain snaking through darkened copper chain acts as a beautiful textured base to support the lovely gemstones and pendant. There is so much color, texture and movement in this simple design. Mix up your techniques and materials for surprising results.

Design Tip

This woven concept works equally well with beaded wire creating a defined S-pattern. Don't be afraid to try techniques using a variety of materials to see what might happen!

MATERIALS

- 1" × 1¼" (2.5cm × 3cm) ceramic peacock feather bead
- 3 green jade freeform polished nuggets
- 3 yellow jasper ovals
- 1½mm natural leather
- 20-gauge annealed iron wire
- 15" (38cm) section aged copper elongated oval chain
- 15¼" (39cm) section color-coated small cable chain in blue
- 2 6mm copper jump ring
- jeweler's glue
- pencil or dowel
- memory wire shears
- round-nose pliers
- 2 pairs chain-nose pliers
- wire cutters

1

2

3

4

5

6

1 Measure and remove chain segments (see Opening and Closing Chain Links on page 22). Attach the blue and copper chains to a 6mm copper jump ring (see Opening and Closing Jump Rings on page 21).

2 The blue chain is going to thread into every third link of the copper chain in an S-pattern. (The blue chain should be threading into the copper from the opposite side each time.)

3 Secure the ends of the threaded chains on the second 6mm copper jump ring.

4 Make a wrapped hook with an approximately 2" (5cm) piece of iron wire (see Making a Wrapped Wire Hook on page 19).

5 At one end of the necklace, knot the end of a 6" (15cm) segment of leather to the 6mm jump ring. Thread a green bead onto the leather. Knot the leather to secure the bead.

6 Repeat step 5 with a second green bead, three yellow beads and a third and final green bead. Knot the leather end onto the hook and cut off any excess leather.

Design Tip

Gemstone bead openings are inconsistent in size. Buy more beads than you'll need to ensure you'll have enough that can thread onto the leather. You can also opt to ream the bead holes larger, but be careful not to force it too much or the bead may break.

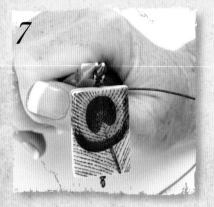

7 Dab both knots with glue and allow to dry. Thread a 4" (10.25cm) segment of steel wire into the pendant. Create a small loop on one end with the round-nose pliers; then create a loosely wrapped coil top (see Making a Wrapped Loo on page 14). Use memory wire shears to cut the excess wire.

8 Using the chain-nose pliers, attach the pendant to the side of the necklace with the copper jump ring.

Fashion forward

Nights in Carthage By Andrew Thornton

What is the same? The patterned, rectangular focal pendant similarly gives thematic tone, as well as directs the eye and parallels the arabesque shape of the hook. The asymmetrical design is the same, including a row of stones on the left and chain on the right. The chain is also dealt with in a similar way, weaving the chain with another material. Another likeness is where the piece hooks together.

What is different? The basic color palette is different. Nights in Carthage uses more earth tones. Since the focal is more monochromatic than Nights in Tunisia, a brighter green nugget attaches the pendant to the necklace, drawing more attention to the focal piece. The wire-wrapped dangles balance the piece and draw further attention toward the focal of the necklace. Rougher stones are used for a more organic feel. Seed beads are used in place of the leather, but gives the same textural vibe.

Jelly Bean Bracelet

A colorful cluster of yummy jelly bean beads looks good enough to eat. This is an explosion of color on your wrist, one that's flirty and fun to wear. For those days when you're feeling playful, this is your bracelet!

MATERIALS

1 center-drilled blue Jangles button bead

5 HHH Enterprises aqua blue jelly bean jade beads

5 HHH Enterprises orchid pink jelly bean jade beads

5 HHH Enterprises orange jelly bean jade beads

5 HHH Enterprises yellow jelly bean jade beads

5 HHH Enterprises red jelly bean jade beads

1½mm leather

25 silver-plated head pins

jeweler's glue

round-nose pliers

chain-nose pliers

wire cutters

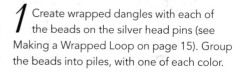

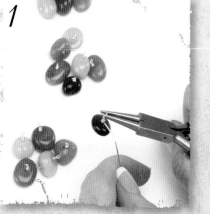

1

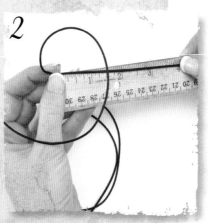

2

3

4

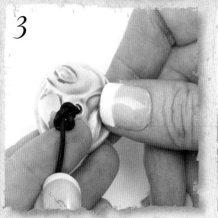

Placement note: step images

5

6

1 Create wrapped dangles with each of the beads on the silver head pins (see Making a Wrapped Loop on page 15). Group the beads into piles, with one of each color.

2 You'll need to adjust the length of the leather to fit your wrist. Start with a 12" (30.5cm) segment so you have room for adjusting. Remember that leather stretches when worn, so err on the tighter side.

3 Make a double knot on one end of the leather. Slide the leather into the hole in the button. Make a knot.

4 Make another knot about approximately 2½" (6cm) down the length of leather.

5 Slide the groups of beads onto the leather, one bead at a time.

6 Repeat using the pattern you created until you reach the final bead.

7 Knot the leather flush against the final bead.

8 Move down about 2½″ (6.25cm) (again adjusting for your wrist size) and create a loop. Use a surgeon's knot to secure the loop; to do this, tie one overhand knot with two wraps and pull tight, then another overhand knot.

9 Dab the knots with jeweler's glue and allow the glue to dry before wearing.

Opulence By Brenda Pinnick

What is the same? I clustered the beads from a core.

What is different? I used flat beads instead of rounded beads and a reversible fabric base. Instead of a bracelet, I made a necklace. The color palette I used is tonal rather than multishaded, focusing on shades of blue.

Chapter 6

Focal Elements

One of the easiest ways to become instantly inspired is with a great focal bead. So many incredibly talented bead artists are out there making beads with inspired colors, patterns, textures and themes. Simply walk a bead show if you want to fill up with ideas. A great way to learn how to think like an artist is to find inspiration in one who has fine-tuned her aesthetic. Acquire some great focal beads, put them into your bead stash and let them guide your work.

In this chapter, we'll create designs inspired by fabulous focals. I'll show you how to pull different elements from them to use in your designs. You'll see how changing the focal bead can greatly influence the design concept. We'll play with all of the new skills you've acquired to create a design dialogue with the artists who create the beads and your work.

There is nothing more inspiring than the joyful expression of art, and we're going to play freely. Grab your bead boards and your pliers, and let's get to the business of design play!

"The soul of art is inspiration." Ginia A. Davis

Chagall Necklace

This incredible hand-painted bead from Russia is a reproduction of a segment of a painting by the artist Marc Chagall. Look closely to appreciate all of the fascinating detail the artist managed to get into this one segment. I pulled my design ideas directly from elements on the pendant: the rickrack trim mimics the zigzag stripe at the top and the pearls and CRYSTALLIZED-Swarovski beads work back to the floral details. I left the vivid blue on the pendant to stand alone in a simple palette of black, white and silver.

Design Tip

Look to the materials for inspiration. There is an endless supply of great art beads out there, and they'll prove instrumental in guiding your work if you let them.

MATERIALS

6 3mm freshwater pearls

8 3mm jet AB CRYSTALLIZED-Swarovski Elements rounds

1 hand-painted Russian Chagall focal pendant from Art Beads

2 4-link and 1 3-link section of Quick Links diamond chain

1 small open center Quick Links circle

black small rickrack trim (or other black cord)

6 6mm silver-plated jump rings

2" (5cm) silver-plated head pin

fabric glue (optional)

round-nose pliers

2 pairs chain-nose pliers

wire cutters

1 Cut off two 23" (58.5cm) segments of rickrack trim. Thread and secure the center of each segment into a diamond link on a 4-link chain segment as shown.

2 Add knots to the end of each cord. You may apply a dab of fabric glue to prevent fraying.

3 Thread a jet bead, the Russian pendant and a second jet bead on a 2" (5cm) head pin and loop the top to make a pendant (see Turning a Loop on page 14).

4 Attached to the end of each rickrack-chain piece is a Quick Links connector. Open a jump ring (see Opening and Closing Jump Rings on page 21) and thread on a Quick Links connector, the pendant and the remaining Quick Links connector. Use the 2 pairs of chain-nose pliers to close the jump ring.

5 Create wrapped dangles with the remaining beads and head pins (see Making a Wrapped Loop on page 15). Attach three wrapped jet beads to the first link on the chain on the left with a jump ring. Add three pearls to the second link and three jet beads to the third link using jump rings.

6

6 Attach the 3-link chain segment on a jump ring to the first link on the right side of the chain.

7 Attach three wrapped pearls and the small Quick Links circle to a jump ring on the end of the 3-link chain.

7

Fashion forward

Peekaboo, I See You

What is the same? The same basic silhouette is used, but with a far more distressed and vintage vibe.

What is different? I decoupaged a vintage image on the back of an antique keyhole to use as the focal element. I added keys, faux pearls, crystals and gemstones. Instead of rickrack, I used rattail in black satin and opted for gunmetal instead of silver chain. Everything changes when you use a different focal element!

Feelin' Groovy Necklace

A stunning floral ceramic bead from Golem inspired this rich and earthy design. I love the way the small green jade discs—wire-wrapped and strung between the beads—look like paddles. The smooth stone beads are so unexpected, and the patina changes as you wear them. I'm very pleased with this design, and I think you'll find it pleasing, too.

Design Tip

When working from a focal bead, don't feel obligated to use all of the colors or to stay within the theme. Use it as a springboard for your creativity and not a set of rules you must slavishly follow.

MATERIALS

- 1 Golem ceramic floral focal bead
- 12 18mm stone coin beads
- 16 8mm carnelian faceted coin beads
- 35 6mm acid green jade coin beads
- 18-gauge silver-plated Artistic Wire
- 20-gauge silver-plated ColourCraft wire
- 27 24-gauge sterling silver head pins
- 49-strand .018 Beadalon wire
- 2 sterling silver EZ-Crimp ends
- 1 sterling silver EZ-Lobster clasp
- 6mm silver-plated jump ring
- EZ-Crimp Tool
- round-nose pliers
- 2 pairs chain-nose pliers
- wire cutters

1 Thread a 4" (10cm) segment of 18-gauge wire into the hole at the top of the pendant. Use round-nose pliers to create a small loop at the back of the pendant to secure the wire (see Turning a Loop on page 14).

2 Bend the wire flush to the front of the pendant and create a loop about ¼" (6mm) from the base of the wire.

3 Cut off excess wire and create a loop as shown.

4 Wrap a segment of 20-gauge wire around the stem of the 18-gauge wire for decoration. Cut off any excess wire with the wire cutters, and tuck the tail under with the chain-nose pliers.

5 Create 27 wrapped dangles using the sterling silver head pins and green jade coins (see Making a Wrapped Loop on page 15). Thread an EZ-Crimp on a 20" (51cm) section of beading wire. Slide on the beads in the following order: jade, carnelian, jade, carnelian, three jade on head pins, carnelian, stone.

6 Continue the pattern: carnelian, three jade on head pins, carnelian, stone, jade, stone, jade, stone, three jade on head pins, carnelian, three jade on head pins, stone, carnelian, stone, three jade on head pins, carnelian, ceramic focal pendant, then jade, three jade on head pins, stone, carnelian, stone, carnelian, stone, carnelian, three jade on head pins, carnelian, stone, carnelian, three jade on head pins, carnelian, three jade on head pins, carnelian, stone, jade, stone, carnelian, jade and a final jade.

7 Thread the wire into the EZ-Crimp using chain-nose pliers to pull the wire through. Keep the design rounded and secure the EZ-Crimp end. Cut off the excess wire. Attach the EZ-Lobster clasp to the EZ-Crimp on the right side and a 6mm jump ring to the EZ-Crimp on the left side.

The Road Less Traveled

What is the same? I pulled the color palette from the pendant, used the three paddle-style bead accents and kept the asymmetrical appeal.

What is different? I added chain in the back, used larger beads, including a larger focal with text, and added a gorgeous sterling silver lobster clasp on the side of the design as another focal element. Three beaded dangles provide some movement.

Green Man Necklace

Melanie Brooks has a knack for making beads that feel simultaneously ancient and modern. The rich earthy colors she favors complement every skin tone. Lately she's been exploring steampunk and her work has taken a fascinating new direction. In this case, I let the beads guide me and added plenty of chain for a simultaneously edgy and earthy appeal.

MATERIALS

1 Earthenwood Studio Toolbox Treasure pendant "Change"

4 Earthenwood Studio Toolbox Treasure links in colors that match pendant

1 large green Earthenwood Studio Leafy Charm

4 8mm carnelian rounds

4 8mm green jade beads

4 6mm × 9mm yellow agate oval beads

4 15-link segments, 1 12-link segment, 1 3-link segment and 3 1-link segments of oval cable oxidized brushed silver chain

2 18-link segments antique brushed brass chain

20-gauge brass Artistic Wire

9 silver-plated head pins

round-nose pliers

2 pairs chain-nose pliers

wire cutters

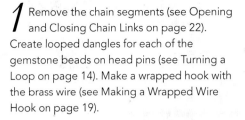

1 Remove the chain segments (see Opening and Closing Chain Links on page 22). Create looped dangles for each of the gemstone beads on head pins (see Turning a Loop on page 14). Make a wrapped hook with the brass wire (see Making a Wrapped Wire Hook on page 19).

2 Attach the pendant to the 3-link segment of silver chain.

3 Attach the chain on both sides to a set of Treasure Links.

4 Attach a second set of Treasure Links to the first set on each side using a single chain link as a jump ring.

5 Fold the brushed brass chains in half. Attach the center link of each folded chain to the final Treasure Link on each side of the Treasure Link chains.

6 On one side of the necklace, attach a chain link into the two chain ends; add the clasp, then close the link.

7

8

9

10

7 Attach the final link of the 12-link silver chain segment through the two brass chain ends on the other side of the necklace.

8 Attach the leaf charm to the end of the 12-link segment.

9 Create the swags by attaching the 15-link silver chain segments to the outer loops on each side of each Treasure Link pair. They should hang below any core chains. Repeat for all bead groups.

10 Attach a green bead dangle to the third link from the top of the chain swag. Attach a yellow bead dangle to the seventh link from the top of the chain swag. Attach a carnelian bead dangle to the tenth link from the top of the chain swag. Repeat this step for all of the chain swags.

Sweet Dreams By Melissa J. Lee

What is the same? I wanted to retain the feel of the ceramic beads in the original, so I used a large ceramic disc with a crescent design by Diane Hawkey as the focal element. I also reproduced the overall shape of the piece: swags hanging from around the ceramic beads, and the back of the necklace keeps a simple line.

What is different? I wanted to create a fantasy-themed necklace as a counterpoint to the steampunk feel of the original piece. The overall color and theme of the focal element and other beads I selected is very tranquil and soft. I further softened the effect by replacing the chain in the original with pearls and silk ribbon. Crystal beads in place of polished stones give the piece a more ornate, fairy-tale quality.

Fashion forward

Love Hurts Earrings

Copper is a soft and malleable substance, and is the perfect material for novice metalworkers. These metal donuts are transformed into tiny works of art with a ball-peen hammer and some text. Wire is wrapped and bent around the bottom half of the design and accented with a hint of sparkle. Love may hurt, but wearing these earrings surely won't!

1. Texture both sides of the copper donut using the round end of a ball-peen hammer and a steel bench block (see Hammering Texture Into Wire and Metal on page 14). Place the donut on the steel bench block and strike the top of the letter stamps with the hammer to engrave the word "LOVE" on the donut.

2. Use the marker to mark the center bottom of the stamped donut and add a mark approximately ¼" (6mm) from the center on each side.

3. Use the larger dowel on the two-hole punch to pierce a hole in the center marked spot on the donut. Repeat using the smaller dowel for the other marked areas.

4. Mark and punch a hole in the center top of the donut.

5. Stamp an 'X' on one heart and an 'O' on the other using the hammer and the steel block.

6. Tightly wrap wire around the center section of the donut three times.

7. Leaving larger spaces, continue wrapping around the bottom of the donut until you reach the center of the other side. Wrap this three times tightly so it's symmetrical with the other side.

8. Wrap one end of the 10" (25.5cm) wire around the left side of a donut adding on two Indian red beads before wrapping the wire tightly one more time to secure.

9 The wire should face the back of the hole in the donut. Slide on a khaki, a smoky quartz and a khaki crystal bicone.

10 Wrap the wire around the other side of the frame, adding two Indian red crystal beads before you secure the wire tightly to the back of the donut.

11 To further secure the wires and add texture, use the round-nose pliers to bend the wires at the front of the donut.

12 Attach the ear wires to the donut.

13 Create double-looped dangles with two 4mm Indian red crystal bicones and two 4mm khaki crystal bicones (see Turning a Loop on page 14).

14 Attach the heart charms to the center bottom hole of the earring using a jump ring. Place an Indian red crystal on one side and a khaki on the other with a jump ring (see Opening and Closing Jump Rings on page 21).

Repeat steps 1–14 to make the second earring.

Protected By Tonia Davenport

Fashion forward

What is the same? I incorporated noticeable texture by etching the Plexiglas, and feature wrapped wire elements.

What is different? Plastic replaces metal. Also, in Margot's design, the wire is wrapped from the cutout hole to the outside; in my interpretation, the wire is wrapped across the cutout opening.

Hypnotique Bracelet

Jennifer Heynen's whimsical beads never fail to make me smile. I brought out their edgier side with annealed iron wire for a cutting-edge look. I've intentionally made the wire organically imperfect. The wire spring was a happy accident; it just worked so well with the spirals on the beads. You have to love when that happens.

MATERIALS

1 1" (2.5cm) yellow Jangles button bead

1 1" (2.5cm) spiral black and white Jangles button bead

1 ¾" (2cm) spiral black-and -white Jangles button bead

20-gauge annealed iron wire

5mm gunmetal jump ring

jump ring maker tool with a 6mm dowel

pencil

memory wire shears

round-nose pliers

chain-nose pliers

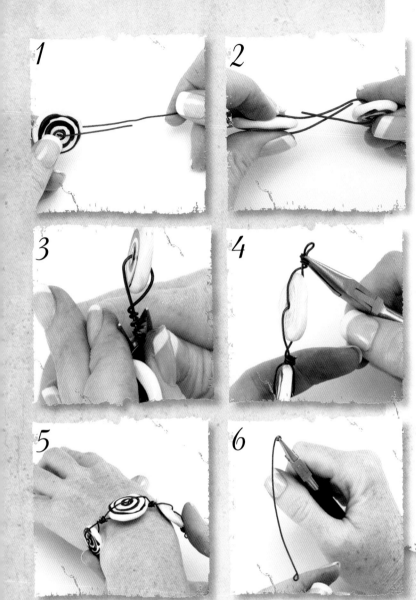

1 Thread the hole of the 1" (3cm) spiral bead with a 4" (10cm) segment of wire. Bend the center of the wire so the 2 ends are flush to the top and bottom of the bead.

2 Thread the opposite end of the wire through the other ¾" (2cm) spiral bead.

3 Use the chain-nose pliers to help wrap the wire tail around the core as shown. Clip off excess wire with the wire cutter. Use the chain-nose pliers to help tuck in the tail.
  Repeat this step to connect the yellow bead and the 1" (3cm) spiral bead.

4 Thread a 3" (7.5cm) segment of wire through yellow bead. Create a loop in one end, organically wrapping the tail around the core using pliers to assist (see Making a Wrapped Loop on page 15). Repeat this step for the ¾" (2cm) spiral bead.

5 Gently bend this section over your wrist, shaping it into an arc.

6 Create an S-hook using a 3½" (9cm) segment of wire. Use the tip of the round-nose pliers to create tiny loops in each wire end (see Turning a Loop on page 14).

7 Bend the wire over the pencil to create the S-shape. Use your fingers to manipulate the wire into final it's shape.

8 Use the jump ring maker tool to create a 1¾" (4.5cm) wire coil. Bend the ends into loops with the chain-nose pliers as shown.

9 Attach one end of the coil to the yellow bead with a jump ring. Attach the other end to the S-hook. Add a jump ring to the end of the ¾" (2cm) spiral bead. Use the S-hook to clasp and unclasp the bracelet.

Fashion forward

Button Box By Barbe Saint John

What is the same? I used the same wire spiral shape and wire wrapping technique.

What is different? I used vintage plastic buttons as the focal beads and separated the coil a bit to make it look like loose thread. I also created a hook clasp rather than an S-clasp.

Steampunk Bracelet

Melanie Brooks' steampunk-influenced ceramic connector inspired this striking mélange of chains and the modified hook clasp. A lone gear adds a touch of movement. Somehow this bracelet manages to be simultaneously tough and tender, and it's sure to inspire some interesting conversations.

MATERIALS

- 1 Earthenwood Studio Openwork Eshutcheon Keyhole Pendant
- 1 Tim Holtz antique bronze sprocket
- 2 3-link and a single link segment Blue Moon Beads large open antique bronze chain
- 3-link and 7-link segments of elongated oval Blue Moon Beads antique bronze chain
- 20-gauge annealed iron wire
- 18-gauge annealed iron wire
- jump ring maker tool
- pencil
- memory wire shears
- round-nose pliers
- 2 pairs chain-nose pliers

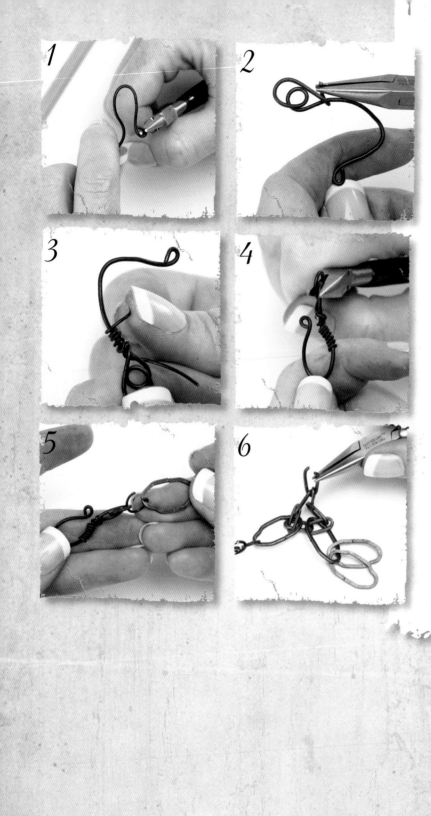

1 Cut a 4" (10cm) segment of 18-gauge wire. Bend the center of the wire over the pencil. Use round-nose pliers to make a small loop in one end (see Turning a Loop on page 14). Use the pliers and your fingers to manipulate the wire into a hook shape.

2 At the bottom of the hook shape, create a loop in the center section of the wire. Wrap the loop around itself creating an eye. Using the chain-nose pliers, wrap the wire tail tightly up around the core wire.

3 Cut a 1" (2.5cm) piece of the 20-gauge wire. Wrap this wire around the base of the hook as shown (see Wrapping Wire Around a Base on page 16). Use the wire cutters to trim the excess wire.

4 Make adjustments to the hook using the chain-nose pliers.

5 Use the jump ring maker tool to create one 10mm 20-gauge jump ring (see Making Jump Rings on page 20). Attach the jump rings to the hook and through a large brass link (see Opening and Closing Jump Rings on page 21).

6 Thread the smaller 7-link segment of chain onto the brass link and into the center of a 3-link segment of the large brass links (see Opening and Closing Chain Links on page 22). Attach the ends of the smaller chain to form a chain loop.

7 Attach the 2 exposed ends of the large 3-link chain segment to the 2-hole side of the focal piece.

8 Attach one end of a three link segment of chain to the 1-hole side of the focal piece.

9 Attach a 3-link segment of smaller chain to the exposed end of the larger chain.

10 Add the sprocket to the other end of the chain.

Escutcheon Elegance
By Melanie Brooks

What is the same? I used the same pendant and similar heavy, aged brass chain with components that look like hardware store items.

What is different? I wanted to make a necklace that looked like it might match the bracelet with more detail and a little bit of color. I included some gunmetal with the brass to get a mixed-metal look.

Resources

ARTBEADS.COM
Jewelry-Making Supplies
www.artbeads.com
1.866.715.BEAD

AUNTIE'S BEADS
Jewelry-Making Supplies
www.auntiesbeads.com
1.866.26.BEADS

BEADALON
Wire, Findings, Stringing Materials
www.beadalon.com
1.866.423.2325

BEADS WORLD, INC.
Beads and Jewelry-Making Supplies
www.beadsworldusa.com
212.302.1199

BLUE MOON BEADS
Beads and Bead Supplies
www.creativityinc.com/
   bluemoonbeads
1.800.727.2727

CREATE YOUR STYLE WITH
CRYSTALLIZED-*SWAROVSKI
ELEMENTS*
Crystal Beads and Components
www.create-your-style.com

DIANE HAWKEY
Handcrafted Ceramic Beads
248.541.0211
www.dianehawkey.com

EARTHENWOOD STUDIO
Handcrafted Porcelain Beads,
Charms and Pendants
www.earthenwoodstudio.com

FUSION BEADS
Jewelry-Making Supplies
www.fusionbeads.com
1.888.781.3559

GREEN GIRL STUDIOS
Handcrafted Pewter and Metal
Beads, Charms and Pendants
www.greengirlstudios.com

HHH ENTERPRISES
Beads, Jewelry and Mixed-Media
Supplies
www.hhhenterprises.com
1.800.777.0218

ILOVETOCREATE
General Crafts, Ceramic Supplies,
Glues and Adhesives
www.ilovetocreate.com
1.800.438.6226

JANGLES BEADS
Handcrafted Ceramic Beads,
Pendants and Charms
www.jangles.net
1.706.207.9032

LILLYPILLY DESIGNS
Laser Inscribed Wood and
Shell Beads
www.lillypillydesigns.com
1.303.543.8673

METALLIFEROUS
Beads, findings, chain, metal and
Jewelry-Making Supplies
www.metalliferous.com
1.888.944.0909

ORNAMENTEA
Jewelry-Making and Mixed-Media
Supplies
www.ornamentea.com
1.919.834.6260

PHOENIX JEWELRY AND PARTS
Beads and Jewelry Supplies
www.phoenixbeads.com
1.212.278.8688

PLAID
Beads and General Crafts Supplies
www.plaidonline.com
1.800.842.4197

RAVEN'S JOURNEY
Jewelry-Making Supplies
www.theravenstore.com

RINGS & THINGS
Beads and Jewelry-Making Supplies
www.rings-things.com
1.800.366.2156

THE BEADIN' PATH
Vintage and New Beads and
Jewelry-Making Supplies
www.beadinpath.com
877.92.BEADS

YORK NOVELTY IMPORTS, INC.
Czech Glass Beads
www.yorkbeads.com
212.594.7040

Index

Even more inspiration

Bead and Wire Jewelry Exposed

Margot Potter, Fernando DaSilva and Katie Hacker

Bead & Wire Jewelry Exposed features over 50 high-fashion jewelry pieces made using techniques that reveal typically hidden components. Beading wire, cording, findings, tubing and chain take center stage in these clever and designs. Each of the three authors, Margot Potter, Katie Hacker and Fernando DaSilva, puts his or her spin on the exposed-element designs, so there's something for everyone.

paperback with flaps;
8.75" × 10.875";
144 pages; Z2508
ISBN-10: 1-60061-159-1
ISBN-13: 978-1-60061-159-9

Beyond The Bead

Margot Potter

If you are a restlessly creative do-it-yourself type, you've found your book. Impatient Beader Margot Potter grabs inspiration from bead making, scrapbooking and mixed-media artistry and brings it together in one book all about wearing your work. *Beyond the Bead* features 26 step-by-step jewelry projects that will teach you a variety of mixed-media techniques and show you an inspired use of supplies. Multiple variations and gallery projects will show you that creativity has no boundaries.

paperback;
8.25" × 10.875";
128 pages; Z2066
ISBN-10: 1-60061-105-2
ISBN-13: 978-1-60061-105-6

A Bead In Time

Lisa Crone

Dip into your life and memories for jewelry inspiration. In *A Bead in Time*, Lisa Crone takes you step-by-step through 35 photo-inspired jewelry projects while giving you tips on how to design pieces based on your own life. You'll learn a range of beading and jewelry techniques, including wire wrapping, peyote stitch, macramé and more. Whether you're a beading beginner or an experienced jewelry crafter, you can get started transforming life into art.

paperback;
8.25" × 10.875";
128 pages; Z2912
ISBN-10: 1-60061-310-1
ISBN-13: 978-1-60061-310-4

These and other fine North Light titles are available at your local craft retailer, bookstore or online supplier, or visit our Web site at www.mycraftivitystore.com.